Practice Workbook

PASO A PASO

1

Mary Louise Carey
Natick High School
Natick, MA

JoAnn DiGiandomenico
Natick High School
Natick, MA

Scott Foresman

Editorial Offices: Glenview, Illinois

Regional Offices: Sunnyvale, California • Atlanta, Georgia
Glenview, Illinois • Oakland, New Jersey • Dallas, Texas

ISBN: 0-673-21681-0

24-VHG-07 06 05 04

FRONT COVER: ©Suzanne Murphy/FPG International
BACK COVER: ©Suzanne Murphy/FPG International

El Primer Paso

It is the first day of school in the city of Madrid, where you are an exchange student for the semester. Many of the students in the class are new to the school, so the teacher has given you time to introduce yourselves. First fill in the lists in the chart. Then complete the dialogues by using words from the lists.

Greetings / responses	Words to talk about names	Words to talk about feelings

1. **A.** —¡Hola! ¿ _____ ?

    B. —Me llamo Tere. ¿Y tú?

    A. — _____ Toño.

    B. —Mucho gusto, Toño.

    A. — _____ , Tere.

2. **A.** — _____ . ¿Cómo te llamas?

    B. — _____ Lupe. ¿Y tú?

    A. —Me llamo Pedro. ¿ _____ , Lupe?

    B. —Muy bien, _____ . ¿Y tú?

    A. — _____ .

Now create your own dialogue.

3. **A.** — _____ .

    B. — _____ .

    A. — _____ .

    B. — _____ .

    A. — _____ .

EL PRIMER PASO

As exchange students, you are all anxious to find out where everyone in the class is from. Fill in the chart using words and expressions, including those you learned from the previous lesson. Then complete the dialogues.

Greetings / responses	Words to talk about where you are from	Words to talk about feelings	Words to say good-by

1. **A.** — _____ , señor Ramírez. Me llamo Ceci.

   B. —Mucho gusto, Ceci. ¿De _____ ? ¿De Chile?

   A. —No, _____ Estados Unidos. ¿Y Ud.?

   B. —Soy de Argentina.

   A. —Adiós, profesor.

   B. — _____ , Ceci.

2. **A.** — _____ , Miguel.

   B. —Hola, Anita. ¿ _____ ?

   A. —Así, así. ¿Y tú?

   B. — _____ .

   A. —¿Eres de Cuba?

   B. —Sí, _____ Cuba. ¿Y tú?

   A. —Soy de Ecuador.

Now create your own dialogue.

3. **A.** — _____ .

   B. — _____ .

   A. — _____ .

   B. — _____ .

You and your family are going to host an exchange student next semester. This student will go to all of your classes with you. In preparation for this, the students in your class are trying to learn some Spanish. Complete the dialogues by identifying the pictures. Follow the model.

—¿Cómo se dice "*table*" en español?

—(<u>Mesa</u> / Pupitre).

1.

—¿Cómo se dice "*book*" en español?

—(Pizarra / Libro).

2.

—¿Cómo se dice "*pen*" en español?

—(Compañero / Bolígrafo).

3.

—¿Cómo se dice "*classmates*" en español?

—(Compañeros / Sala de clases).

4.

—¿Cómo se dice "*student*" en español?

—(Pupitre / Estudiante).

5.

—¿Cómo se dice "*sheet of paper*" en español?

—(Hoja de papel / Pizarra).

6.

—¿Cómo se dice "*female teacher*" en español?

—(Profesora / Compañera).

7.

—¿Cómo se dice "*student desk*" en español?

—(Pupitre / Pizarra).

8.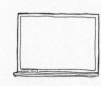

—¿Cómo se dice "*chalkboard*" en español?

—(Profesor / Pizarra).

EL PRIMER PASO

Everyone you talk to today is trying to determine their schedule for the week. Some people are very mixed up about the days and dates, while others seem to be very organized. Complete each dialogue by referring to the calendar. Follow the models.

julio						
lunes	martes	miércoles	jueves	viernes	sábado	domingo
				1	2	3
4	5	6	7	8	9	10
11	12	13	14	15	16	17
18	19	20	21	22	23	24
25	26	27	28	29	30	31

—Hoy es el cinco de julio.
—¿Es jueves?
—*No, es martes.*

—Hoy es el ocho de julio.
—¿Es viernes?
—*Sí, es viernes.*

1. —Hoy es el treinta de julio.

   —¿Es lunes?

   — _____ .

2. —Hoy es el trece de julio.

   —¿Es domingo?

   — _____ .

3. —Hoy es el veintiuno de julio.

   —¿Es jueves?

   — _____ .

4. —Hoy es el once de julio.

   —¿Es lunes?

   — _____ .

5. —Hoy es el primero de julio.

   —¿Es martes?

   — _____ .

6. —Hoy es el doce de julio.

   —¿Es sábado?

   — _____ .

Your group of friends is trying to decide if they can have just one birthday party this year to celebrate everyone's birthday. You ask when each person's birthday is, hoping that the dates are close to each other. Find each person's birthday on the calendar. Then complete each dialogue by writing the date in Spanish. Follow the model.

enero						
l	m	m	j	v	s	d
8	*9	10	11	•12	13	14

*Felipe   •Jaime

agosto						
l	m	m	j	v	s	d
16	17	*18	19	20	•21	22

*Luz   •Emilio

marzo						
l	m	m	j	v	s	d
*27	28	29	30	•31		

*Mónica   •Rocío

septiembre						
l	m	m	j	v	s	d
*1	2	3	4	5	•6	7

*Agustín   •Irene

—¿Cuándo es el cumpleaños de Rocío?

—*Es el treinta y uno de marzo.*

1. —¿Cuándo es el cumpleaños de Felipe?

   — _____ .

2. —¿Cuándo es el cumpleaños de Agustín?

   — _____ .

3. —¿Cuándo es el cumpleaños de Irene?

   — _____ .

4. —¿Cuándo es el cumpleaños de Mónica?

   — _____ .

5. —¿Cuándo es el cumpleaños de Jaime?

   — _____ .

6. —¿Cuándo es el cumpleaños de Luz?

   — _____ .

Your school has scheduled some repairs to be done in your classroom. As a result, you and your classmates are helping your teacher to pack up supplies. Complete each dialogue by finding the correct picture and writing the corresponding number. Follow the model.

 25

 1

 31

16

8

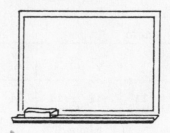 19

—¿Cuántos libros hay?

—Hay *veinticinco.*

1. —¿Cuántos pupitres hay?

   —Hay _____ .

2. —¿Cuántas hojas de papel hay?

   —Hay _____ .

3. —¿Cuántas pizarras hay?

   —Hay _____ .

4. —¿Cuántos bolígrafos hay?

   —Hay _____ .

5. —¿Cuántas mesas hay?

   —Hay _____ .

Everyone is trying to figure out the new student teacher. He seems nice enough, but he is constantly giving orders during the class. You and your friends decide to review Spanish commands after school so that you will be better able to follow his orders. Complete each dialogue by choosing an answer from the list below. Follow the model.

Siéntate, por favor.	Pasa a la pizarra, por favor.	Abran el libro.
Levántate, por favor.	Repitan, por favor.	Date la vuelta.
Silencio, por favor.	Trabajen con un compañero.	Presta atención.

—¿Cómo se dice *"stand up"* en español?

—*Levántate, por favor.*

1. —¿Cómo se dice *"be quiet"* en español?

   — _____ .

2. —¿Cómo se dice *"open the book"* en español?

   — _____ .

3. —¿Cómo se dice *"repeat"* en español?

   — _____ .

4. —¿Cómo se dice *"work with a classmate"* en español?

   — _____ .

5. —¿Cómo se dice *"sit down"* en español?

   — _____ .

6. —¿Cómo se dice *"turn around"* en español?

   — _____ .

7. —¿Cómo se dice *"go to the chalkboard"* en español?

   — _____ .

8. —¿Cómo se dice *"pay attention"* en español?

   — _____ .

EL PRIMER PASO

Fecha _____

Everyone seems restless in school today. The teacher is being bombarded with questions! Complete each dialogue by matching the picture with the expressions below. Follow the model.

ir a la oficina del director	abrir la ventana	ir al armario	cerrar la ventana
ir a la oficina de la directora	ir al baño	sacarle punta a mi lápiz	

—¿Puedo *ir al baño?*
—Sí, ve.

1.

—¿Puedo _____ ?
—Claro.

2.

—¿Puedo _____ ?
—No, lo siento.

3.

—¿Puedo _____ ?
—Sí, ábrela.

4.

—¿Puedo _____ ?
—Ahora no.

5.

—¿Puedo _____ ?
—Sí, ciérrala.

El Primer Paso

Your little brother is in first grade and he is having his first quiz tomorrow. Your mother has asked you to help him review for it. Complete the dialogues by using the expressions you have learned in this chapter. Follow the model.

—¿Cómo se dice "*table*" en español?

—*Mesa.*

1. —¿Cómo te llamas?

   — _____ .

2. —¿Cómo estás?

   — _____ .

3. —¿De dónde eres?

   — _____ .

4. —¿Cómo se dice "*chalkboard*" en español?

   — _____ .

5. —¿Cuántos años tienes?

   — _____ .

6. —¿Cuál es tu número de teléfono?

   — _____ .

7. —¿Cuál es la fecha de hoy?

   — _____ .

8. —¿Cómo se dice "*pen*" en español?

   — _____ .

9. —¿Qué día es hoy? ¿Y mañana?

   — _____ .

10. —¿Cuántos días hay en una semana?

    — _____ .

11. —¿Cuántas semanas hay en un mes?

    — _____ .

12. —¿Cómo se dice "*student desk*" en español?

    — _____ .

El Primer Paso

Vocabulary

Words to talk about names

_____

_____

Words to tell how you feel

_____

_____

Words to greet and to say good-by

_____

_____

_____

_____

_____

_____

Words to ask for and to give information

_____

_____

_____

_____

_____

_____

Days of the week

_____

_____

_____

_____

_____

Months of the year

_____   _____

_____   _____

_____   _____

_____   _____

_____   _____

Words to say when something takes place

_____

_____

Words to acknowledge instructions

_____

_____

Paso a paso 1

EL PRIMER PASO

Nombre _____

Fecha _____

**Practice Workbook
Organizer**

Numbers   Classroom objects

_____   _____

_____   _____

_____   _____

_____   _____

_____   _____

_____   _____

_____   _____

_____   _____

1. Use _____ to show respect when speaking to an older person.

2. Use _____ when speaking to someone your own age or when you are being friendly.

3. _____ , _____ , _____ , and _____ all mean *the*.

4. Most nouns ending in *-o* and *-os* are _____ .

5. Most nouns ending in *-a* and *-as* are _____ .

6. Spanish calendars begin the week with _____ and end with

   _____ .

7. In Spanish, dates are formed by using _____ + _____ +

   _____ + _____ .

8. _____ means "first." We use the regular numbers for the other numbers

   in a date.

9. Days of the week and months of the year are *not* _____

   _____ .

Some new students in your English class are talking about their pastimes. Based on the pictures, select the sentence you think they are saying and circle the corresponding letter.

1. a. Me gusta estudiar.
b. Me gusta tocar la guitarra.
c. Me gusta nadar.

2. a. Me gusta dibujar.
b. Me gusta tocar la guitarra.
c. Me gusta patinar.

3. a. No me gusta leer.
b. No me gusta practicar deportes.
c. No me gusta ayudar en casa.

4. a. Me gusta practicar deportes.
b. Me gusta ver la tele.
c. Me gusta estudiar.

5. a. No me gusta patinar.
b. No me gusta ver la televisión.
c. No me gusta dibujar.

6. a. Me gusta hablar por teléfono.
b. Me gusta leer.
c. Me gusta cocinar.

7. a. Me gusta ir a la escuela.
b. Me gusta escuchar música.
c. Me gusta nadar.

8. a. No me gusta patinar.
b. No me gusta ir al cine.
c. No me gusta nadar.

At a family gathering, you see relatives whom you haven't seen for a long time. You and your cousins are interested in finding out about each other. Look at the pictures and write out which activity each person prefers to do. Follow the model.

RAÚL ¿Qué te gusta más, practicar deportes o ayudar en casa?

ANA *Pues, me gusta más practicar deportes.*

1. **ELISA** ¿Qué te gusta más, escuchar música o hablar por teléfono?

LUIS _____.

2.  **ÓSCAR** ¿Qué te gusta más, ir al cine o dibujar?

ANA _____.

3. **ROSA** ¿Qué te gusta más, nadar o ir a la escuela?

MARIO _____.

4. **LAURA** ¿Qué te gusta más, ver la televisión o leer?

PABLO _____.

5. **PACO** ¿Qué te gusta más, patinar o estudiar?

LUCI _____.

6.  **DAVID** ¿Qué te gusta más, escuchar música o cocinar?

SOFÍA _____.

You are interviewing some new students from Nicaragua for the school newspaper. When you tell them about the activities you enjoy or do not enjoy, they respond by giving you their opinion of these activities. Follow the models.

—A mí me gusta *nadar.* ¿Y a ti?
—*Pues, a mí también.*

—No me gusta mucho *estudiar.* ¿Y a ti?
—*Pues, a mí no me gusta tampoco.*

1.

—No me gusta _____ . ¿Y a ti?

— _____ .

4.

—No me gusta _____ . ¿Y a ti?

— _____ .

2.

—A mí me gusta _____ . ¿Y a ti?

— _____ .

5.

—A mí me gusta _____ . ¿Y a ti?

— _____ .

3.

—A mí me gusta _____ . ¿Y a ti?

— _____ .

6.

—No me gusta mucho _____ . ¿Y a ti?

— _____ .

Vocabulario para conversar   **15**

People know things about us because of the activities we like or dislike. Complete the statements by underlining the correct word from the two choices in parentheses. Follow the model.

No me gusta hablar por teléfono.

Soy (sociable / <u>callada</u>).

1. Me gusta practicar deportes.

    Soy (artístico / deportista).

2. No me gusta ayudar en casa.

    Soy (trabajadora / perezosa).

3. Me gusta dibujar.

    Soy (generosa / artística).

4. Me gusta ir a la escuela.

    Soy (trabajador / tacaño).

5. Me gusta nadar y patinar.

    Soy (perezosa / deportista).

6. Me gusta hablar con amigos.

    Soy (sociable / desordenada).

7. Me gusta tocar la guitarra.

    Soy (prudente / artístico).

8. No me gusta cocinar.

    Soy (gracioso / perezoso).

9. Me gusta ayudar en casa.

    Soy (trabajadora / atrevida).

10. Me gusta estudiar.

    Soy (perezosa / trabajadora).

Laura and Pedro have a new guidance counselor at school who wants to find out more about the students. Answer the questions according to the pictures. Follow the model.

—¿Cómo eres, ordenado o desordenado?

—*Soy desordenado.*

1.  —¿Cómo eres, generosa o tacaña?

   — _____ .

2. —¿Cómo eres, serio o gracioso?

   — _____ .

3. —¿Cómo eres, deportista o artístico?

   — _____ .

4. —¿Cómo eres, perezosa o trabajadora?

   — _____ .

5. —¿Cómo eres, impaciente o paciente?

   — _____ .

Now, use three adjectives to describe yourself.

Soy _____ , _____ y _____ .

Gramática en contexto / Los adjetivos   **17**

Even though they are best friends, Carmen and Tomás are opposites. Complete their conversation according to the pictures. Follow the model.

CARMEN	¿Cómo eres?
TOMÁS	*Soy gracioso.*
CARMEN	*¿De veras? Yo soy seria.*

1.

TOMÁS	¿Cómo eres?
CARMEN	_____
TOMÁS	_____

4.

TOMÁS	¿Cómo eres?
CARMEN	_____
TOMÁS	_____

2.

CARMEN	¿Cómo eres?
TOMÁS	_____
CARMEN	_____

5.

CARMEN	¿Cómo eres?
TOMÁS	_____
CARMEN	_____

3.

CARMEN	¿Cómo eres?
TOMÁS	_____
CARMEN	_____

6.

TOMÁS	¿Cómo eres?
CARMEN	_____
TOMÁS	_____

18 *Gramática en contexto / Los adjetivos*

A The students on the debate team are trying to pair up for their next competition. They want to see who has similar personality traits. Answer each question with the opposite of the underlined word. Follow the model, but pay attention to the endings.

DIEGO   Yo soy <u>ordenado</u>. ¿Y tú?

INÉS   Yo soy *desordenada*.

CAROLINA   Yo soy <u>seria</u>. ¿Y tú?

RICARDO   Yo soy _____1_____ .

RAMÓN   Yo soy <u>trabajador</u>. ¿Y tú?

JAIME   Yo soy _____2_____ .

EDUARDO   Yo soy <u>paciente</u>. ¿Y tú?

CARLOTA   Yo soy _____3_____ .

JUANA   Yo soy <u>atrevida</u>. ¿Y tú?

TERESA   Yo soy _____4_____ .

SARA   Yo soy <u>callada</u>. ¿Y tú?

JAVIER   Yo soy _____5_____ .

B You are writing an article for your school newspaper about the foreign student exchange program. Some of the exchange students have described themselves. Use these descriptions to decide each student's personality trait and write the correct word.

ANDRÉS   No soy ordenado. Soy _____1_____ .

LUIS   Yo no soy tacaño. Soy _____2_____ .

MARCOS   Me gusta ayudar en casa. Soy _____3_____ .

MARIANA   No me gusta trabajar mucho. Soy _____4_____ .

SANDRA   Me gusta mucho dibujar. Soy _____5_____ .

ALBERTO   Me gusta practicar deportes. Soy _____6_____ .

Gramática en contexto / Los adjetivos   **19**

CAPÍTULO 1

Your friend is in a bad mood and is giving a negative response to everything you ask. Complete the conversation according to the pictures. Follow the models.

—¿Te gusta *cocinar* o *patinar*?
—*No me gusta ni cocinar ni patinar.*

—¿Eres *generoso* o *tacaño*?
—*No soy ni generoso ni tacaño.*

1.

—¿Eres _____ o _____ ?

— _____ .

4.

—¿Eres _____ o _____ ?

— _____ .

2.

—¿Te gusta _____ o _____ ?

— _____ .

5.

—¿Te gusta _____ o _____ ?

— _____ .

3.

—¿Te gusta _____ o _____ ?

— _____ .

6.

—¿Eres _____ o _____ ?

— _____ .

You've just met Margarita and she is telling you what activities she does not enjoy. Based on the pictures, write what she is saying, then answer her according to how you really feel about each activity. Follow the model.

—*A mí no me gusta cocinar. ¿Y a ti?*

—*Pues, a mí sí me gusta.*

o: —*A mí no me gusta tampoco.*

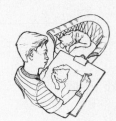

4.

— _____

— _____ .

1.

— _____

— _____ .

5.

— _____

— _____ .

2.

— _____

— _____ .

6.

— _____

— _____ .

3.

— _____

— _____ .

7.

— _____

— _____ .

Paso a paso 1

Nombre _____

CAPÍTULO 1

Fecha _____

Practice Workbook
Organizer

I. Vocabulary

Activities I like to do

_____   _____

_____   _____

_____   _____

Activities others might like to do

_____   _____

_____   _____

_____

Words that help me say what I like to do

_____   _____

_____   _____

_____   _____

Words that help me say what I don't like to do

_____   _____

_____   _____

_____   _____

Words that say what I am like

_____   _____

_____   _____

_____   _____

Words that ask what others like to do

_____   _____

_____   _____

Words that ask someone what he or she is like

_____   _____

_____   _____

Words that describe me or others

_____   _____

_____   _____

_____   _____

_____   _____

_____   _____

II. Grammar

1. Adjectives describing females usually end in _____ . Adjectives describing males usually end in _____ . Adjectives that end in -e can describe _____ .

2. If you do not like either of two choices, use: _____ .

3. Use _____ to contrast something you like with something you or someone else dislikes. Use _____ to agree with someone who dislikes something.

Your schedule for the school year has been posted. Check to see what time your classes will meet.
Circle the letter of the statement that best matches the picture. Follow the model.

Horario		
	Primer semestre	**Segundo semestre**
(1ª) primera hora	matemáticas	inglés
(2ª) segunda hora	inglés	matemáticas
(3ª) tercera hora	educación física	ciencias de la salud
(4ª) cuarta hora	ciencias sociales	ciencias sociales
(5ª) quinta hora	almuerzo	almuerzo
(6ª) sexta hora	arte	música
(7ª) séptima hora	español	ciencias
(8ª) octava hora	ciencias	español

a. Tengo matemáticas en la primera hora.
b. Tengo matemáticas en la cuarta hora.
c. Tengo ciencias en la cuarta hora.

1. a. Tengo español en la segunda hora.
    b. Tengo inglés en la tercera hora.
    c. Tengo inglés en la segunda hora.

2. a. Tengo música en la sexta hora.
    b. Tengo música en la séptima hora.
    c. Tengo arte en la séptima hora.

3. a. Tengo el almuerzo en la cuarta hora.
    b. Tengo el almuerzo en la quinta hora.
    c. Tengo ciencias en la quinta hora.

4. a. Tengo arte en la tercera hora.
    b. Tengo ciencias en la octava hora.
    c. Tengo ciencias sociales en la sexta hora.

5. a. Tengo arte en la quinta hora.
    b. Tengo arte en la tercera hora.
    c. Tengo arte en la sexta hora.

6. a. Tengo ciencias sociales en la cuarta hora.
    b. Tengo ciencias de la salud en la segunda hora.
    c. Tengo ciencias de la salud en la primera hora.

Because you are disorganized, sometimes your mother checks to see if you have all of your supplies for the school day. Complete each conversation by identifying the pictures. Follow the model.

—¿Qué necesitas para la clase de inglés? *¿Una regla?*

—No. Necesito una regla para la clase de *matemáticas*.

1.

—¿Qué necesitas para la clase de ciencias?

¿ _____ ?

—No. Necesito_____ .

2.

—¿Qué necesitas para la clase de educación física?

¿ _____ ?

—No. Necesito_____ .

3.

—¿Qué necesitas para la clase de ciencias?

¿ _____ ?

—No. Necesito_____ .

4.

—¿Qué necesitas para la clase de matemáticas?

¿ _____ ?

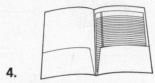

—No. Necesito_____ .

5.

—¿Qué necesitas para la clase de música?

¿ _____ ?

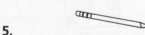

—No. Necesito_____ .

6.

—¿Qué necesitas para la clase de arte?

¿ _____ ?

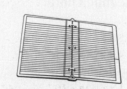

—No. Necesito_____ .

You've lost your book bag, so you are going to have to borrow books from your friend all day. You have to find out what time each of your friend's classes begins and ends so that you can return the books. Complete the conversation by underlining the correct answer. Follow the model.

—¿A qué hora empieza tu clase de español?

—Empieza (a las dos / a las doce).

1.

—¿A qué hora empieza tu clase de inglés?

—Empieza (a las diez / a la una).

2.

—¿A qué hora empieza tu clase de matemáticas?

—Empieza (a las once y quince / a las dos y cuarto).

3.

—¿A qué hora empieza tu clase de ciencias?

—Empieza (a la una / a las once).

4.

—¿A qué hora termina tu clase de arte?

—Termina (a las dos y treinta y cinco / a las dos y cuarenta y cinco).

5.

—¿A qué hora empieza tu clase de música?

—Empieza (a las dos y treinta / a las doce y media).

6.

—¿A qué hora termina tu clase de ciencias de la salud?

—Termina (a las ocho y cincuenta y dos / a las dos y cincuenta y ocho).

Vocabulario para conversar   **25**

A reporter for the school newspaper is taking a poll and needs to know when each of your classes begins and ends. Answer each question according to the times given. Follow the model.

| 2:00 | 2:40 |

—¿Cuándo empieza y termina tu clase de ciencias?

—*Empieza a las dos y termina a las dos y cuarenta.*

Son las diez y cuarenta y cinco   o   Son cuarto para las once

1. | 10:15 | 11:00 |

—¿Cuándo empieza y termina tu clase de arte?

— Empieza a las diez y cuarto y termina a las once

2. | 8:45 | 9:30 |

—¿Cuándo empieza y termina tu clase de español?

— Empieza a las cuarto para las nueve y termina a las nueve y media

3. | 12:00 | 12:50 |

—¿Cuándo empieza y termina tu clase de inglés?

— Empieza a las doce y termina a las diez para la una.

4. | 7:55 | 8:30 |

—¿Cuándo empieza y termina tu clase de matemáticas?

— Empieza a las cinco para las ocho. y termina a las ocho y media

5. | 1:10 | 1:35 |

—¿Cuándo empieza y termina tu clase de ciencias sociales?

— Empieza a las una y diez y termina a las veinte y cinco para las dos

6. | 9:20 | 10:10 |

—¿Cuándo empieza y termina tu clase de educación física?

— Empieza a las nueve y veinte y termina a las diez y diez

Paso a paso 1   Nombre _____

CAPÍTULO 2   Fecha _____   Practice Workbook **2-5**

The students in your class are discussing the activities they like to do. Based on the question and on the last letter(s) of the underlined word, complete the answers using the appropriate subject pronoun. Follow the model. Complete the verb chart before you start.

-ar Verbs

yo	nad-_____	nosotros nosotras	nad-_____
tú	nad-_____	vosotros vosotras	nadáis
Ud. él ella	nad-_____	Uds. ellos ellas	nad-_____

—Ramón y Beatriz nadan. ¿Y tú?

—*Yo* <u>nado</u> también.

1. —Gloria y Rosa patinan. ¿Y Verónica?

    — _____ <u>patina</u> también.

2. —Yo ayudo en casa. ¿Y Anita y Miguel?

    — _____ <u>ayudan</u> en casa también.

3. —Tú practicas deportes en la clase de educación física. ¿Y Esteban?

    — _____ <u>practica</u> deportes en la clase de educación física también.

4. —Ud. escucha música. ¿Y Uds.?

    — _____ <u>escuchamos</u> música también.

5. —Mercedes y Rosa dibujan en la clase de arte. ¿Y Raúl?

    — _____ <u>dibuja</u> en la clase de arte también.

6. —Yo toco la guitarra. ¿Y Rita?

    — _____ <u>toca</u> la guitarra también.

7. —Ricardo y yo estudiamos mucho en la clase de español. ¿Y Ana y Susana?

    — _____ <u>estudian</u> mucho en la clase de español también.

Gramática en contexto / Los pronombres personales   **27**

You and your friends are going around town asking for donations for the local charity. Tell which form of the word "you"—*tú, usted (Ud.),* or *ustedes (Uds.)*—you would use to address each of these people. Follow the model.

YOUR FAVORITE AUNT   **TÚ** or **USTED**

1. the school principal   _____

2. all the Spanish teachers   _____

3. your cousin who is the same age as you _____

4. your aunt and uncle   _____

5. the police chief   _____

6. your favorite neighbor   _____

7. your friend's mother   _____

8. the president of the bank   _____

9. the school superintendent and his secretary _____

10. your father   _____

11. the members of the soccer team   _____

12. your brother   _____

Everyone is at the school store looking for the supplies they need. Tell which supplies they need by adding the appropriate form of the verb *necesitar,* followed by the name of the object in the picture. Follow the model. Complete the verb chart before you start.

-ar Verbs

yo	*necesit-_____*	nosotros nosotras	*necesit-_____*
tú	*necesit-_____*	vosotros vosotras	necesitáis
Ud. él ella	*necesit-_____*	Uds. ellos ellas	*necesit-_____*

  Roberto *necesita una mochila.*

1.  (Nosotros) _____.

2.   Alicia _____.

3.   (Yo) _____.

4.   José y Mercedes _____.

5.   (Tú) _____.

6.   Ellos _____.

Gramática en contexto / Verbos que terminan en -ar   **29**

You are talking about the things you do and don't do in your different classes. Complete each sentence by identifying the picture and using the correct form of the appropriate verb. Follow the model. Complete the verb chart before you start.

-ar Verbs

yo	mir- _____	nosotros nosotras	mir- _____
tú	mir- _____	vosotros vosotras	miráis
Ud. él ella	mir- _____	Uds. ellos ellas	mir- _____

   Roberto *no habla por teléfono* en la clase de arte.

1.    Yo _____ en la clase de inglés.

2.    Antonio y Daniela _____ en la clase
de matemáticas.

3.    Tú _____ en la clase de música.

4.    Carmen y yo _____ en la clase de arte.

5.    Yo _____ en la clase de ciencias sociales.

6.    María _____ en la clase de ciencias
de la salud.

It's the first day of school and your mother is checking to make sure that you have all the supplies you need for your classes. Complete the sentences by using *el* or *la*. Follow the model.

¿Tienes *el* bolígrafo?

1. ¿Tienes _____ mochila?

2. ¿Tienes _____ calculadora en la mochila?

3. ¿Tienes _____ diccionario de español?

4. ¿Tienes _____ carpeta de argollas?

5. ¿Tienes _____ regla para la clase de matemáticas?

6. ¿Necesitas _____ libro de ciencias?

7. Tú necesitas _____ papel para dibujar.

8. ¿Tienes _____ tarea?

Now complete each sentence by using *un* or *una*.

9. ¿Necesitas _____ grabadora en la clase de música?

10. ¿Y _____ guitarra?

11. ¿Necesitas _____ cuaderno y _____ lápiz en la clase de inglés?

12. ¿Tienes _____ marcador?

I. Vocabulary

School subjects that I find easy

_____   _____

_____   _____

_____

School subjects that I find hard

_____   _____

_____   _____

School supplies

_____   _____

_____   _____

Words that indicate location

_____   _____

_____   _____

Words that ask and tell when something takes place

_____   _____

_____   _____

_____   _____

Words that ask and tell time

_____   _____

_____   _____

_____   _____

Words that express quantity, regret, and hesitation

_____   _____

_____   _____

_____   _____

Words that ask for information

_____   _____

_____   _____

II. Grammar

1. Words that tell who performs an action

Singular	Singular	Plural	Plural
			vosotros

2. What are the *-ar* verb endings?

Singular	Plural
nad-____	*nad-_____*
nad-____	nadáis
nad-____	*nad-____*

3. Most masculine nouns end in _____ . Most feminine nouns end in _____ .

It's a beautiful day and you can't decide what to do. You need a friend to help you make the decision. Complete the conversations by underlining the correct answer. Follow the model.

—¿Te gusta más ir al campo o ir a la playa?

—Me gusta más ir (<u>a la playa</u> / al campo).

1.

—¿Te gusta más ir al gimnasio o ir al parque?

—Me gusta más ir (<u>al gimnasio</u> / al parque).

2.

—¿Te gusta más ir a la piscina o ir al parque de diversiones?

—Me gusta más ir (a la piscina / <u>al parque de diversiones</u>).

3.

—¿Te gusta más ir al centro comercial o ir al campo?

—Me gusta más ir (al <u>centro comercial</u> / al campo).

4.

—¿Te gusta más ir a la playa o ir a la piscina?

—Me gusta más ir (a la playa / <u>a la piscina</u>).

5.

—¿Te gusta más ir al parque o ir al campo?

—Me gusta más ir (al parque / <u>al campo</u>).

6.

—¿Te gusta más ir al parque de diversiones o ir al parque?

—Me gusta más ir (al parque de diversiones / <u>al parque</u>).

A new student has arrived from Cuba. She is curious to know at what time of year you do certain activities. Complete the conversations according to the pictures. Follow the model.

—¿Cuándo vas *al parque*?

—Generalmente, voy en *el otoño*.

1.

—¿Cuándo vas __al playa__ ?

—Generalmente, voy en __el verano__ .

2.

—¿Cuándo vas __al parque de diversiones__

—Generalmente, voy en __la primavera__ .

3.

—¿Cuándo vas __al gimnasio__ ?

—Generalmente, voy en __el invierno__ .

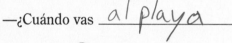

4.

—¿Cuándo vas __al campo__ ?

—Generalmente, voy en __la primavera__ .

5.

—¿Cuándo vas __al centro comercial__

—Generalmente, voy en __el otoño__ .

6.

—¿Cuándo vas __al piscina__ ?

—Generalmente, voy en __el verano__ .

34 *Vocabulario para conversar*

You've been sick for a week and now you can't wait to get out and do something! It seems, however, that all of your friends are now starting to show symptoms of your illness. Complete the conversation by underlining the correct expressions. Follow the model.

—Juan, ¿te gustaría (ir de compras / <u>ir a una fiesta</u>)?

—No, no puedo. (<u>Estoy cansado</u>. / Estoy cansada.)

1.

—Rosa, ¿te gustaría (<u>jugar tenis</u> / ir de compras)?

—No, no puedo. (<u>Estoy enferma</u>. / Estoy enfermo.)

2.

—Mario, ¿te gustaría (ir de compras / <u>jugar videojuegos</u>)?

—No, no puedo. (Estoy ocupada. / <u>Estoy ocupado</u>.)

3.

—Fernando, ¿te gustaría (<u>ir de compras</u> / ver la tele)?

—No, no puedo. (Estoy cansada. / <u>Estoy cansado</u>.)

4.

—Alberto, ¿te gustaría (ir a una fiesta / <u>ir de pesca</u>)?

—No, no puedo. (<u>Estoy ocupado</u>. / Estoy ocupada.)

5.

—Susana, ¿te gustaría (<u>jugar béisbol</u> / jugar videojuegos)?

—No, no puedo. (Estoy enfermo. / <u>Estoy enferma</u>.)

6.

—Eduardo, ¿te gustaría (ir de pesca / <u>ver la tele</u>)?

—No, no puedo. (<u>Estoy ocupado</u>. / Estoy ocupada.)

You are asking your friends to join you in doing some activities. They all want to, but they have other responsibilities. Complete the conversation according to the pictures. Follow the model.

—¿Quieres *practicar deportes?*

—Quiero, pero no puedo. Necesito *ayudar en casa.*

1.

—¿Quieres **ir a pescar** ?

—Quiero, pero no puedo. Necesito **ir de compras**.

2.

—¿Quieres **Jugar video Juegos** ?

—Quiero, pero no puedo. Necesito **ir a nadar** .

3.

—¿Quieres **ir a una fiesta** ?

—Quiero, pero no puedo. Necesito **ir a estudiar** .

4.

—¿Quieres **escuchar musica** ?

—Quiero, pero no puedo. Necesito **ir a leer** .

5.

—¿Quieres **ir a patinar** ?

—Quiero, pero no puedo. Necesito **ir a escuela** .

6.

—¿Quieres **hablar en el telefono** ?

—Quiero, pero no puedo. Necesito **ayudar en la casa**

The weekend has nearly arrived and everyone is making plans. Complete the conversation with the correct form of the verb *ir*. Follow the model. Complete the verb chart before you start.

Ir

yo	v- *voy*	nosotros nosotras	v- *vamos*	
tú	v- *vas*	vosotros vosotras	vais	
Ud. él ella	v- *va*	Uds. ellos ellas	v- *van*	

—¿Adónde *vas* tú?

—Yo *voy* a la piscina.

1. —¿Adónde _____ *van* _____ Uds.?
   —Nosotros _____ *vamos* _____ al parque.

2. —Mi familia _____ *van* _____ a ir de compras. ¿Y tú?
   —Yo _____ *voy* _____ a ir al campo.

3. —¿Adónde _____ *va* _____ Esteban el sábado?
   —Él _____ *va* _____ al gimnasio el sábado.

4. —¿Adónde _____ *van* _____ Rosa y José el lunes?
   —Ellos _____ *van* _____ a la playa.

5. —Yo _____ *voy* _____ a ir a una fiesta el viernes. ¿Y Uds.?
   —Nosotras _____ *vamos* _____ a ayudar en casa.

6. —Lucía y Juana _____ *van* _____ a jugar videojuegos. ¿Y Sara?
   —Ella _____ *va* _____ a jugar básquetbol.

7. —¿Adónde _____ *van* _____ Mariana y Enrique?
   —Ellos _____ *van* _____ al parque de diversiones.

8. —Diego _____ *va* _____ a ir a la playa en el verano. ¿Y Uds.?
   —David y yo _____ *vamos* _____ a ir al campo.

 Paso a paso 1 | **Nombre** _____

CAPÍTULO 3

Fecha _____

 Practice Workbook **3-6**

It's Thursday night and everyone is making plans for what they will do Friday afternoon after their classes are over. Complete the conversations by identifying the pictures and by using the correct forms of the verb *ir.* Follow the model. Complete the verb chart before you start.

Ir

yo	v- *voy*	nosotros / nosotras	v- *vamos*
tú	v- *vas*	vosotros / vosotras	vais
Ud. / él / ella	v- *va*	Uds. / ellos / ellas	v- *van*

—Yo *voy a nadar* después de las clases. ¿Y Raquel?

—Raquel *va a estudiar.*

1.

—Margarita *va a patinar* . ¿Y Uds.?

—Nosotros *vamos a pescar* .

2.

—Él *va a jugar deportes* ? ¿Y Jaime?

—Jaime *va a dibujar* .

3.

—Nosotros *vamos a jugar videojuegos* ? ¿Y tú?

—Yo *voy a leer* .

4.

—Rafael *va a jugar footbol* . ¿Y Ana y Juan?

—Ellos *van a ayudar en la casa*

5.

—Salvador y Rosa *van al cine* . ¿Y Uds.?

—Elena y yo *vamos de compras* .

a l = a t e l

38 *Gramática en contexto / Ir + a + infinitivo*

 Copyright © Scott, Foresman and Company

A It's an unusual Saturday night because everyone has a car and can participate in the activities they enjoy with different friends. Complete each response using the preposition *con* and the correct pronoun. Follow the model.

—¿Puedes ir de compras conmigo?

—Sí, puedo ir de compras *contigo*.

1. —¿Puedes practicar deportes con Inés y Clara?

   —Sí, puedo practicar deportes *con ellas y Clara* .

2. —¿Carlota va a la piscina contigo?

   —Sí, Carlota va a la piscina *conmigo* .

3. —¿Puedo ir con Uds.?

   —Sí, puedes ir *con nosotros* .

4. —¿Te gustaría estudiar con Claudia?

   —Sí, me gustaría estudiar *con ella* .

5. —¿Te gustaría ir al parque conmigo?

   —Sí, me gustaría ir *contigo* .

B You are in charge of making sure that everyone on your team has a ride to the soccer game. You're checking to see that each person knows who they are going with. Complete each response using *con* and the correct pronoun. Follow the model.

—¿Con quién vas? ¿Con María?

—Sí, voy *con ella*.

1. —¿Con quién van Manuel y Diego? ¿Con Paco?

   —Sí, ellos van *con él* .

2. —¿Con quién va Eduardo? ¿Contigo?

   —No, no va *conmigo* .

3. —¿Con quién vas tú? ¿Con Bárbara y María?

   —Sí, voy *con ellas* .

4. —¿Con quién voy? ¿Con Clara, Marta y Rafael?

   —No, no vas *con ellos* .

5. —¿Con quién vamos nosotros? ¿Con Isabel y Beatriz?

   —Sí, Uds. van *con ellas* .

Gramática en contexto / La preposición con   **39**

You have been away on vacation. Now that you're back, you're anxious to find out where everyone is and how they are doing. Complete each conversation with the correct form of the verb *estar*. Follow the model. Complete the verb chart before you start.

Estar

yo	est- _____		nosotros nosotras	est- _____
tú	est- _____		vosotros vosotras	estáis
Ud. él ella	est- _____		Uds. ellos ellas	est- _____

—¿Dónde *está* Alejandro?

—Alejandro *está* en el campo.

1. —¿Dónde _____ Rosalinda y Tomás?

   —Ellos _____ en la piscina.

2. —¿ _____ tú ocupado?

   —Sí, yo _____ ocupado.

3. —¿Dónde _____ Susana?

   —Ella _____ en el centro comercial.

4. —¿Dónde _____ María, Rosa y Alicia?

   —Ellas _____ en el gimnasio.

5. —¿ _____ Salvador cansado?

   —Sí, él _____ cansado.

6. —¿ _____ Inés enferma?

   —Sí, Inés _____ enferma.

7. —¿Dónde _____ Ud.?

   —Yo _____ en casa.

8. —¿Dónde _____ tú y Juanita?

   —Juanita y yo _____ en el campo.

The exchange student from Peru who stayed with you last year is back visiting for a few days. He was hoping to see some of the people he met when he was here before, but they all seem to be away. Write a dialogue according to the pictures, using the correct form of the verb *estar.* Follow the model. Complete the verb chart before you start.

Estar

yo	est- _____	nosotros nosotras	est- _____
tú	est- _____	vosotros vosotras	estáis
Ud. él ella	est- _____	Uds. ellos ellas	est- _____

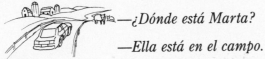

—¿Dónde está Marta?

—Ella está en el campo.

Marta

1. —¿ _____ ?

   — _____ .

   Teresa y Paula

2. —¿ _____ ?

   — _____ .

   La familia

3. —¿ _____ ?

   — _____ .

   tú

4. —¿ _____ ?

   — _____ .

   tú y Mariana

5. —¿ _____ ?

   — _____ .

   Raúl, Clara y Elena

Gramática en contexto / El verbo estar   **41**

Nombre _____

Fecha _____

I. Vocabulary

Places to go	Activities	Seasons	Days of the week

II. Grammar

1. The verb *to go:* _____

   S _____ P _____

   _____ _____

   _____ vais

   _____ _____

2. When people are going to do something
   you should use the correct form of:

   _____ .

3. When people are going to a place
   you should use the correct form of:

   _____ .

4. Verb used to express where people are or how they feel: _____

   S _____ P _____

   _____ _____

   _____ estáis

   _____ _____

5. When doing things with other people you should use: _____ .

   S _____ P _____

   _____ _____

   _____ con vosotros(as)

   _____ _____

   _____ _____

It is getting close to lunchtime and you and your friends can't help discussing food! Based on the pictures, circle the letter that corresponds to the correct answer. Follow the model.

¿Qué comes en el desayuno, huevos o jamón?
    (a.) Generalmente como huevos.
    b. Generalmente como jamón.

1. ¿Qué prefieres comer, sandwiches
   o hamburguesas?
    a. Prefiero comer sandwiches.
    b. Prefiero comer hamburguesas.

4. ¿Qué prefieres comer en la cena, pescado
   o queso?
    a. Prefiero comer pescado.
    b. Prefiero comer queso.

2. ¿Te gusta el arroz o el cereal?
    a. Me encanta el arroz.
    b. Me encanta el cereal.

5. ¿Qué te gustan más, las ensaladas o las
   papas fritas?
    a. Me encantan las ensaladas.
    b. Me encantan las papas fritas.

3. ¿Qué te gusta más, el bistec o el pollo?
    a. Me gusta más el bistec.
    b. Me gusta más el pollo.

6. ¿Qué te gusta más, el pan o la sopa
   de verduras?
    a. Me gusta más el pan.
    b. Me gusta más la sopa de verduras.

Eduardo and his friends can't decide what kind of restaurant to go to Friday night. So on Thursday, they ask each other what foods they like to cook and eat at home. Complete each sentence by writing the name of the food in the picture. Follow the model.

—¿Qué comes en el almuerzo?

—Yo como una *sopa de verduras.*

1.

—¿Qué vas a cocinar en la cena?

—Yo voy a cocinar _____ .

2.

—¿Qué prefieres comer en el desayuno?

—Yo prefiero comer _____ .

3.

—¿Qué te encanta comer en el almuerzo?

—Me encanta comer _____ .

4.

—¿Qué quieres con el cereal?

—Yo quiero _____ .

5.

—¿Qué te gusta comer con las papas al horno?

—Me gusta comer _____ .

6.

—¿Qué comes en el desayuno?

—Generalmente, yo como _____ .

7.

—¿Qué prefieres cocinar en el almuerzo?

—Yo prefiero cocinar _____ .

8.

—¿Qué quieres comer en el almuerzo?

—Yo quiero comer _____ .

It's the hottest day of the summer and everyone just wants to eat and drink things that are cool and refreshing. Complete each dialogue by underlining the correct answer. Follow the model.

—¿Qué prefieres beber, agua o limonada?

—Prefiero beber (<u>agua</u> / limonada).

1.

—¿Qué te gustaría comer, una zanahoria o un tomate?

—Me gustaría comer (una zanahoria / un tomate).

2.

—¿Tienes sed?

—Sí. Me encanta (la limonada / el jugo de naranja).

3.

—¿Qué frutas prefieres, las manzanas o los plátanos?

—Prefiero (las manzanas / los plátanos).

4.

—¿Qué te gustan más, las cebollas o los guisantes?

—Me gustan más (las cebollas / los guisantes).

5.

—¿Qué te gustaría beber, café o té helado?

—Me gustaría beber (café / té helado).

6.

—¿Qué te gustan más, las naranjas o las uvas?

—Me gustan más (las naranjas / las uvas).

7.

—¿Qué debo comer en el almuerzo?

—Debes comer (judías verdes / lechuga).

Vocabulario para conversar   **45**

CAPÍTULO 4

You have to write a report about food for your health class. Interview some of your classmates to see which foods and beverages they like. Complete each conversation by writing the names of the foods or drinks in the pictures. Follow the model.

—¿Qué prefieres comer?

—Prefiero comer *plátanos* y *uvas*.

1.

—¿Qué bebes en el desayuno, leche o jugo de naranja?

—Bebo _____ . Es muy sabroso.

2.

—¿Qué comes en la ensalada?

—Generalmente como _____ y _____ .

3.

—¿Qué comes con el bistec?

—Yo como _____ y _____ .

4.

—¿Qué prefieres beber, café o té?

—Prefiero beber _____ .

5.

—¿Qué bebes con los sandwiches?

—Yo bebo _____ y a veces _____ .

6. ![apples and oranges]

—¿Debes comer frutas? ¿Por qué?

—Sí. Debo comer _____ y _____ .
Son buenas para la salud.

A You are at a restaurant with your friends Ana and Gabriel. You want to find out if they like to eat the things you are thinking of ordering. Complete each conversation by adding the definite article *los* or *las*. Follow the model.

—Gabriel, ¿te gustan *las* zanahorias en una ensalada?

—Sí, me gustan mucho.

1. —Y a ti, Ana, ¿te gustan _____ papas fritas en el almuerzo?

    —Sí, a veces.

2. —Ana, ¿te gustan _____ refrescos con un sandwich?

    —No, nunca.

3. —Gabriel, ¿te gustan _____ huevos con pan tostado?

    —Sí, son muy sabrosos.

4. —Ana, ¿te gustan _____ frutas en el desayuno?

    —No, a mí no me gustan.

5. —Y a ti, Gabriel, ¿te gustan _____ plátanos en el desayuno?

    —A mí sí me gustan.

B Now Ana wants to find out what you like to eat. Complete your answers to her questions according to what you see in the pictures.

—*Las papas fritas* son sabrosas, ¿verdad?

—Sí, pero no son buenas para la salud.

1.  —¿Te gustan _____ en la sopa?

    —Más o menos.

2.  —¿Te gustan _____ con el bistec?

    —No, son horribles.

3.  —¿Qué te gusta comer con el pollo?

    —Me encantan _____ .

4. —¿Te gustan _____ con la hamburguesa?

    —No, no me gustan nada. Son horribles.

5. —¿Te gustan _____ por la mañana?

    —No. ¡Qué asco!

Gramática en contexto / El plural de los sustantivos　　**47**

Capítulo 4

A Your health teacher is doing a unit on nutrition. At the end of class, she asks a lot of questions about the eating habits of the students in the class and also about what some of your classmates are like. Complete the dialogues by using the correct form of the adjective in parentheses. Complete the chart before you start.

Masculine Singular	Feminine Singular	Masculine Plural	Feminine Plural
gracioso	graciosa	graciosos	graciosas
malo	_____	_____	_____
bueno	_____	_____	_____
artístico	_____	_____	_____
deportista	_____	_____	_____
amable	_____	_____	_____

1. —Los plátanos son _____ para la salud, ¿verdad? (bueno)

   —Sí, y las zanahorias son _____ para la salud también.

2. —Las naranjas son _____ , ¿verdad? (sabroso)

   —Sí, y los refrescos son _____ también.

3. —¿Son _____ Paco y Ana? (artístico)

   —Sí, y Rosa y Sara son _____ también.

4. —¿Son _____ Clara y Lucía? (deportista)

   —Sí, y Alfredo y Andrés son _____ también.

B You've invited some friends to your house for lunch. You start out talking about the food and end up talking about your friends' personality traits. Complete each conversation with the correct feminine or masculine form of the underlined adjective. Follow the model.

—El pollo es <u>sabroso</u>. ¿Y la hamburguesa?

—La hamburguesa es *sabrosa* también.

1. —El jamón es <u>malo</u> para la salud. ¿Y la lechuga?

   —¡La lechuga no es _____ para la salud!

2. —Yo estoy <u>cansada</u> ahora. ¿Y Ramón?

   —Ramón está _____ también.

3. —Cecilia es <u>impaciente</u>. ¿Y cómo es Alberto?

   —Alberto es _____ también.

4. —El estudiante es <u>prudente</u>. ¿Y la estudiante?

   —Ella es _____ también.

Paso a paso 1   Nombre _____

CAPÍTULO 4   Fecha _____   Practice Workbook **4-7**

After a long workout, you and your friends are very hungry and thirsty. List what people are eating and drinking by looking at the pictures and by adding the correct form of the verbs *comer* or *beber*. Follow the model. Complete the verb chart before you start.

-er Verbs

yo	com- _____	nosotros nosotras	com- _____
tú	com- _____	vosotros vosotras	coméis
Ud. él ella	com- _____	Uds. ellos ellas	com- _____

   Rosa *come manzanas.*

1.   Luis y Manuel _____ .

2.   Nosotros _____ .

3.   Yo _____ .

4.   Carmen y yo _____ .

5.   Tú _____ .

6.   Uds. _____ .

7.   Ellos _____ .

8.   Usted _____ con _____ .

Gramática en contexto / Verbos que terminan en -er   **49**

A For your health class report, you are interviewing a number of people about what they like to eat and drink. Complete each conversation with the correct form of the underlined verb. Follow the model. Complete the verb chart before you start.

-er Verbs

yo	com- _____	nosotros nosotras	com- _____
tú	com- _____	vosotros vosotras	coméis
Ud. él ella	com- _____	Uds. ellos ellas	com- _____

—¿Qué <u>comen</u> Uds. en el desayuno?

—Nosotros *comemos* pan tostado.

1. —¿Qué <u>bebes</u> en la cena?

   —Yo _____ leche en la cena.

2. —¿Qué <u>come</u> Luis?

   —Luis _____ uvas.

3. —¿Qué <u>beben</u> Uds. en el almuerzo?

   —Nosotros _____ agua en el almuerzo.

4. —¿Qué <u>comen</u> Víctor y Manuel?

   —Ellos _____ hamburguesas.

B Now that you know some of the eating habits of your friends, you also want to express your opinion. Choose the verb that makes the most sense in your statements. Fill in the blank with the correct form of the verb you choose. Follow the model.

Federico *come* (beber / comer) pescado y ensalada.

1. Uds. _____ (deber / beber) comer más verduras. Son buenas para la salud.

2. Yo nunca _____ (beber / comer) té en el desayuno.

3. Javier y yo siempre _____ (comer / beber) agua en la cena.

4. Tú _____ (deber / beber) comer frutas todos los días.

5. Alicia y Blanca nunca _____ (comer / beber) huevos.

6. Tú y Enrique _____ (beber / comer) tomates en la ensalada.

A Today none of your friends want to do any activities by themselves, so they are working in pairs. Draw a line under the correct form of the verb. Follow the model. Complete the verb charts before you start.

	-er Verbs	-ar Verbs
yo	com-_____	nad-_____
tú	com-_____	nad-_____
él / ella / Ud.	com-_____	nad-_____
nosotros / nosotras	com-_____	nad-_____
vosotros / vosotras	coméis	nadáis
ellos / ellas / Uds.	com-_____	nad-_____

Mi amigo y yo (<u>bebemos</u> / beben) limonada.

1. Manuel y María (practican / practico) deportes después de las clases.

2. Tú y Carlota (estudian / estudias) español.

3. ¿Qué (comen / come) Rosario y Andrés en la cena?

4. Mi familia y yo (leemos / leo) mucho por la noche.

5. María y yo (toca / tocamos) la guitarra.

B Now it's your turn to pair up everybody else for the rest of the day. Write the correct form of the verb in parentheses. Follow the model.

Jaime y Mercedes *leen* (leer) un libro.

1. Tú y yo _____ (ayudar) en casa el sábado.

2. Ellos y Mónica _____ (beber) jugo de naranja.

3. Tú y tu amiga _____ (deber) estudiar más.

4. Mis amigos y yo _____ (comer) el almuerzo a las dos.

5. Ana y tú _____ (necesitar) una carpeta de argollas.

Paso a paso 1

CAPÍTULO 4

Nombre

Fecha

Practice Workbook
Organizer

I. Vocabulary

Words that describe or refer to food	Foods	Beverages

II. Grammar

1.

Masculine/feminine, Singular/plural	MS	FS	MP	FP
Definite article				
Indefinite article				

2. Singular nouns that end in the letter *z* change to _____ in the plural.

3. To make an adjective plural, add _____ to the final vowel. If it ends in a consonant, add _____ .

4. Verb endings: *-er*

S   P

_____   _____

_____   _____

_____   -éis

_____   _____

5. Regular *-er* verbs you know

a. _____

b. _____

c. _____

d. _____

6. Rule for forming the 6 forms of regular *-er* verbs:

_____

_____

7. Use *Uds.* when: _____

8. Use *ellos/ellas* when: _____

As Mariana looks through a family picture album, she realizes that she doesn't know many of the people in her extended family. Help her identify each picture by underlining the correct words in the sentence. Follow the model.

Verónica es (<u>la madre</u> / la tía) de Carlos.

mi abuelo
Pedro

mi abuela
Carmen

mi madre
María

mi padre
Luis

mi tía
Verónica

mi tío
Tomás

mi hermano
José

mi hermana
Gabriela

yo
Mariana

mi primo
Carlos

mi prima
Ana

1. Luis es (el hijo / el padre) de Gabriela.

2. Carmen es (la tía / la abuela) de Ana.

3. José es (el hermano / el primo) de Carlos.

4. Yo, Mariana, soy (la tía / la hermana) de José.

5. Ana es (la tía / la prima) de José.

6. Pedro es (el padre / el abuelo) de Mariana.

7. José es (el hermano / el padre) de Gabriela.

8. María es (la madre / la tía) de Carlos.

9. Verónica y Tomás son (los padres / los tíos) de Gabriela.

10. Gabriela es (la hermana / la prima) de José.

Mariana has decided to enlist your help to find out as much information as she can about her family. Refer to the family tree on 5-1. Follow the model.

—¿Cómo se llama *la madre* de Mariana?

—Se llama María.

1. —¿Cómo se llama _____ de José?

   —Se llama Tomás.

2. —¿_____ tiene Verónica?

   —Verónica tiene dos, Carlos y Ana.

3. —¿Cómo se llama _____ de Luis?

   —Se llama José.

4. —¿Es Carlos _____?

   —No, Carlos tiene una hermana, Ana.

5. —Mariana, ¿cómo se llama _____ de José?

   —Se llama Carmen.

6. —José, ¿tienes _____?

   —Sí, tengo dos, Gabriela y Mariana.

7. —¿_____ tiene Mariana?

   —Mariana tiene dos hermanos.

8. —¿Cómo se llaman _____ de Mariana?

   —Se llaman Verónica y Tomás.

9. —¿Cómo se llaman _____ de Mariana?

   —Se llaman María y Luis.

10. —¿Cuántos _____ tienen los padres de José?

    —Ellos tienen tres, Gabriela, José y Mariana.

Blanca, an exchange student from Peru, is showing you pictures of the relatives, friends, and pets she left behind in Lima. The pictures are rather faded and you have to ask her a lot of questions. Refer to the pictures on pages 158–159 in your textbook if you are using Book 1 or pages 200–201 if you are using Book A. Complete her statements by underlining the correct words. Follow the model.

Clara y Claudia (Luz y Luisa) tienen el (<u>pelo negro</u> / pelo rubio).

1. Mi primo Marcos (Jorge) es un muchacho (alto / bajo).

2. Ramón (Agustín) es un hombre (joven / viejo).

3. Mi gato es (pequeño / pequeña).

4. Mi tío Juan (Luis) tiene el (pelo canoso / pelo castaño).

5. El perro de Juan (Luis) es (fea / feo).

6. Mis primos Paco y Pepe (Daniel y David) son (gemelas / gemelos).

7. Ramón (Agustín) tiene el (pelo castaño / pelo canoso).

8. Mi hermana Adela (Rebeca) es una (muchacha / mujer) baja.

9. Daniel (José Luis) es (viejo / joven).

10. Yo creo que Ramón (Agustín) es (guapa / guapo).

11. Daniel (José Luis) es (mayor / menor) que Marcos (Jorge).

12. Mi tía Gloria (Pilar) es (cariñosa / cariñoso).

At a family reunion, you and your cousin realize that many people in the family are opposites.
Complete the chart so that you have the four forms of each adjective. Then answer the questions
by writing the opposite of the underlined word. Follow the model.

Masculine Singular	Feminine Singular	Masculine Plural	Feminine Plural
alto	alta _____	altos _____	altas _____
bajo	_____	_____	_____
viejo	_____	_____	_____
joven	_____	_____	_____
grande	_____	_____	_____

Yo soy <u>alto</u>. ¿Y tú?

Yo soy *bajo*.

1. Mercedes es <u>vieja</u>. ¿Y Esteban?

Esteban es _____.

2. Los perros son <u>feos</u>. ¿Y los gatos?

Los gatos son _____.

3. Ana y Susana son <u>mayores</u>. ¿Y Raúl y Juan?

Ellos son _____.

4. Mi abuela es <u>baja</u>. ¿Y mi abuelo?

Mi abuelo es _____.

5. Mis padres son <u>jóvenes</u>. ¿Y tus padres?

Mis padres son _____.

6. Los gatos son <u>pequeños</u>. ¿Y los perros?

Los perros son _____.

7. Juan es <u>un hombre</u>. ¿Y Gloria?

Gloria es una _____.

8. Adela es <u>una muchacha</u>. ¿Y Marcos?

Marcos es _____.

Marcos wants to be a reporter someday. Meanwhile, every time he meets someone new, he has a million questions for them. Complete the verb chart. Then complete the conversations by using the correct form of *tener*. Be sure to look at the rest of the sentence to give you clues. Follow the model.

Tener

yo	_____	nosotros nosotras	_____
tú	_____	vosotros vosotras	tenéis
Ud. él ella	_____	Uds. ellos ellas	_____

MARCOS	¿Tú *tienes* hermanos?
ROSA	Sí, yo *tengo* tres hermanos.

1.

MARCOS	¿Uds. _____ un perro?
ANA y ROSA	No, no _____ un perro, pero yo _____ un gato.
MARCOS	¿Cuántos años _____ tu gato?
ANA	Mi gato _____ 5 años.

2.

MARCOS	Paula, ¿_____ Ud. abuelos?
PAULA	Sí, yo _____ un abuelo y dos abuelas.
MARCOS	¿Cuántos años _____ su abuelo?
PAULA	Él _____ 76 años.

3.

MARCOS	¿_____ tú un bolígrafo?
SUSANA	No, no _____ un bolígrafo, pero Rafael _____ un lápiz.
MARCOS	¡Gracias! Y ustedes, Esteban y Rosalinda, ¿_____ sus libros de ciencias?
ESTEBAN y ROSALINDA	No, no _____ los libros de ciencias, pero Rosalinda _____ su libro de español.

4.

MARCOS	¿Quién _____ mi cuaderno?
PEDRO	Yo no _____ tu cuaderno, pero sí _____ tu bolígrafo.
MARCOS	Creo que Marina y Lola _____ mi cuaderno.
PEDRO	Creo que sí.

Gramática en contexto / El verbo tener   **57**

You and your friends have known each other since you were little kids. You are alike and different in many ways. Complete the verb chart. Then look at the pictures and complete each conversation by using the correct form of *ser*. Follow the model.

Ser

yo	_____	nosotros nosotras	_____
tú	_____	vosotros vosotras	sois
Ud. él ella	_____	Uds. ellos ellas	_____

—Tú *eres impaciente.* ¿Y Ana?

—*Ella es paciente.*

1. —Gloria _____ . ¿Y Eduardo?

   — _____ .

2. —Tigre _____ . ¿Y Michi?

   — _____ .

3. —Yo _____ . ¿Y Josefina?

   — _____ .

4. —Tú y Fela _____ . ¿Y María y yo?

   — _____ .

5. —Mónica y David _____ . ¿Y ellos?

   — _____ .

You are gathering information about teachers and students for the new in-school cable TV station. Some of the information you receive is from face-to-face interviews. Other information comes from questionnaires people have filled out. Complete the verb chart. Then complete each statement using the correct form of *tener* or *ser*. Follow the model.

	Tener	Ser
yo	_____	_____
tú	_____	_____
él / ella / Ud.	_____	_____
nosotros / nosotras	_____	_____
vosotros / vosotras	tenéis	sois
ellos / ellas / Uds.	_____	_____

Yo *soy* el Sr. Ruiz. Yo *tengo* dos hermanas.

1. ¡Hola, Federico! Tú _____ el amigo de Juan. Tú _____ tres

   hermanos y tú _____ muy paciente. ¿Tú _____ un perro?

   Yo _____ un perro y un gato. Ellos _____ bonitos y graciosos.

2. Me llamo Ángela. Yo _____ el pelo negro y _____ alta. Yo

   _____ una familia grande. _____ cinco hermanos y dos

   hermanas. Todos ellos _____ simpáticos e inteligentes. Mi hermano Juan

   _____ muy guapo. Nosotros _____ un perro muy grande.

3. Yo _____ Mariana y no _____ hermanos. Yo _____

   hija única. Yo _____ dos primos, Ana y Miguel. Ellos _____ muy

   trabajadores y graciosos. Ellos _____ dos perros.

4. Buenos días, Sr. Muñoz. ¿_____ Ud. una familia grande o pequeña? ¿Su esposa

   _____ Sofía? Uds. _____ hijas gemelas, Anita y Mónica. Ellas

   _____ diez años y _____ artísticas y muy bonitas.

It is locker cleanout day, and everyone's belongings have ended up in the middle of the corridor. All of your fellow students are trying to sort through the pile to find their things. Complete the chart of possessive adjectives. Then answer the questions, following the model.

One owner / One thing

_____

_____

_____

One owner / More than one thing

_____

_____

_____

—¿Tienes el libro de Felipe?

—Sí, tengo *su* libro.

1. —¿Dónde está tu lápiz?

    —_____ lápiz está aquí.

2. —¿Tiene Ricardo los bolígrafos de Alicia?

    —No, él no tiene _____ bolígrafos.

3. —¿Es Miriam tu prima?

    —No, ella no es _____ prima.

4. —¿Dónde está mi calculadora?

    —_____ calculadora está aquí.

5. —¿Cómo se llaman tus abuelos?

    —_____ abuelos se llaman Rosita y Ángel.

6. —¿Dónde está la carpeta de José?

    —_____ carpeta está aquí.

7. —¿Son los hijos del señor Rivera?

    —Sí, son _____ hijos.

8. —¿Necesitas mis libros?

    —Sí, necesito _____ libros.

At your family reunion there's great confusion because no one can figure out who is related to whom. Read the rules for forming possessives and then follow the model to complete each statement.

To indicate possession:
1. Use *de* + noun

   or
2. Use *mi(s), tu(s), su(s)* before the noun.

Susana es la hermana de Juan.

Ella *es su* hermana.

1. Tú y Rosa son primos.

   Ella _____ prima.

2. Tú y yo somos primos.

   Tú _____ primo.

3. Ángela es mi madre.

   Yo _____ hija.

4. Ángela es la hermana de Susana y de Juan.

   Susana y Juan _____ tíos.

5. Tú y Antonio son hermanos.

   Él _____ hermano.

6. Pedro es el padre de Juan.

   Pedro _____ padre.

7. Tú y yo somos amigas.

   Tú _____ amiga.

8. Todos nosotros somos una familia.

   Ustedes _____ familia.

In preparation for a family reunion, each member of your family has been asked to write a short paragraph about himself or herself. Complete the verb chart. Then complete each paragraph with the correct form of the appropriate verb.

	Estar	Ir	Tener	Ser
yo	_____	_____	_____	_____
tú	_____	_____	_____	_____
él / ella / Ud.	_____	_____	_____	_____
nosotros / nosotras	_____	_____	_____	_____
vosotros / vosotras	estáis	vais	tenéis	sois
ellos / ellas / Uds.	_____	_____	_____	_____

1. Me llamo Roberto Sánchez Torres. Mi familia _____ a ir a España de

   vacaciones. Ahora nosotros _____ en la escuela porque _____

   primavera. Yo _____ quince años. Yo _____ tres hermanos.

   Mi familia _____ un perro, Chito. Él _____ grande y feo. Él

   _____ perezoso también. Nosotros _____ muchos primos. Ellos

   no _____ a España con nosotros porque ellos _____ ocupados.

2. Me llamo Isabel Torres Hernández. Yo _____ baja y _____

   el pelo castaño. Yo _____ hija única, pero _____ muchos

   primos. Mis primos _____ altos. Nosotros _____ deportistas

   y sociables. Mi primo mayor _____ muy trabajador. Mis primos y

   yo _____ muchos amigos. Nosotros _____ al campo en

   el verano.

3. Me llamo Ana Luisa Torres García. Yo _____ una hermana. Nosotras

   _____ treinta y tres años. Mi hermana y yo _____ gemelas,

   pero yo _____ graciosa y ella _____ seria. En el verano,

   nosotras _____ a la playa. En el invierno, mi familia _____ al

   centro comercial. Cuando mis hijas _____ hambre, ellas _____

   muy impacientes. Y tú, ¿adónde _____ en invierno?

Paso a paso 1

Nombre _____

CAPÍTULO 5

Fecha _____

Practice Workbook
Organizer

I. Vocabulary

Family members	Words that describe people

Other people	Animals	Words to talk about age

II. Grammar

1. The verb *to have:* _____

S	P
_____	_____
_____	tenéis
_____	_____

2. The verb *to be:* _____

S	P
_____	_____
_____	sois
_____	_____

3. Use *tener* to _____

_____ .

4. Use *ser* to _____

_____ .

5. In Spanish, words that show possession are called: _____ .

S	P
_____	_____
_____	_____
_____	_____

A You and your best friend are shopping for school clothes. In the store, the two of you discuss the prices of clothes and how they fit with the salesperson. Identify each picture by underlining the correct word in parentheses. Follow the model.

—¿Cómo te quedan (<u>los zapatos</u> / los pantalones) negros?

—Me quedan bien.

1.

—¿Cuánto cuesta (la camiseta / el suéter) azul?

—Cuesta cuarenta dólares.

2.

—¿Cómo te queda (la falda / la sudadera) roja?

—No me queda bien. Me queda grande.

3.

—¿Cuánto cuestan (los pantalones cortos / la camiseta)?

—Cuestan veinte dólares.

4.

—¿Cómo te quedan (los tenis / los zapatos)?

—Me quedan pequeños.

5.

—¿Cuánto cuestan (las camisetas / los calcetines) verdes?

—Cuestan cinco dólares.

B While in the clothing store, you overhear some of the conversations the salesperson has with other customers. Underline the word in parentheses that best completes the question or answer.

1. —¿Qué ropa (llevas / buscas) cuando vas al campo?

   —Generalmente, los tenis y los pantalones cortos.

2. —¿Cómo te (quedan / queda) la blusa?

   —Bien, gracias.

3. —¿La chaqueta amarilla es para Ud., señor?

   —Sí, la chaqueta es (para ti / para mí).

4. —Señorita, ¿(desea / desean) pantimedias o calcetines?

   —Ni pantimedias ni calcetines, gracias.

5. —¿Cuánto (cuestan / cuesta) esa chaqueta?

   —Sólo treinta dólares.

You are going away during school vacation. You realize that you really don't have anything appropriate to wear. In your local clothing store, you find a very patient salesperson. He keeps asking if he can help you, and he answers all of your questions. Complete each dialogue by:

- identifying the picture
- giving the correct form of the adjective
- giving the correct form of the verb
- writing the dollar amount in words

Be careful when the picture is of more than one thing! It will affect each sentence! Follow the model.

rojo, $25   —¿Qué desea Ud.?

—Me gustaría comprar *la camisa roja*.

Me *queda* bien. ¿Cuánto *cuesta*?

—*Cuesta veinticinco* dólares.

1. **azul, $55**   —¿Qué desea Ud., señorita?

—Me gustaría comprar _____ .

Me _____ bien. ¿Cuánto _____ ?

— _____ dólares.

2. **marrón, $70**   —¿Qué desea Ud., señor?

—Me gustaría comprar _____ .

Me _____ bien. ¿Cuánto _____ ?

— _____ dólares.

3. **amarillo, $28**   —¿Qué desea Ud., señora?

—Me gustaría comprar _____ .

Me _____ bien. ¿Cuánto _____ ?

— _____ dólares.

4. **rosado, $4**   —¿Qué desea Ud., señor?

—Me gustaría comprar _____ .

Me _____ bien. ¿Cuánto _____ ?

— _____ dólares.

Vocabulario para conversar   **65**

A new mall has recently opened in your city. The exchange student who is visiting from Venezuela is amazed at how large it is. As you show her around, she has lots of questions. Complete each sentence by underlining the word that identifies the picture or that best completes the dialogue. Follow the model.

—Me gustan tus zapatos nuevos. ¿Dónde los compraste?

—Los compré en (la tienda de ropa / <u>la zapatería</u>).

1.

—Ese vestido te queda bien. ¿Dónde lo compraste?

—Lo compré en (un almacén / una zapatería).

2.

—Me gustan esos pantalones cortos. ¿Dónde los compraste?

—Los compré en (el almacén / la tienda de descuentos).

3. —Me gusta esa blusa morada. ¿Es (nueva / barata)?

—Sí. Sólo cuesta diez dólares.

4.

—Esas faldas son muy bonitas. ¿Dónde las compraste?

—Las compré en (una tienda de ropa / una tienda de descuentos).

5. —Esa blusa es muy bonita. ¿Es nueva?

—No. La compré (hace / por) dos meses.

6. —Me gusta tu camisa. ¿Es (nueva / vieja)?

—Sí, la compré hace tres días.

7. —¿Cuánto pagaste por el suéter?

—Pagué setenta dólares.

—¡Qué (barato / caro)!

8. —Esos pantalones son nuevos, ¿verdad?

—Sí, los (pagué / compré) hace cinco días.

A You have a job interview and you need something new to wear. You look through your friend's closet for ideas, asking her where she bought things and how much she paid for them. Complete the statements by identifying the pictures. Follow the model.

—¿Dónde compraste tu sudadera?

—La compré en (la / una) *tienda de descuentos.*

1. —¿Dónde compraste tus zapatos azules?

—Los compré en _____ .

2. —¿Dónde compraste tus jeans?

—Los compré en _____ .

3. —¿Dónde compraste esa camiseta verde?

—La compré en _____ .

B Now complete this conversation using the words from the word bank.

pagué	compré	qué barato	este	pagaste	ganga

1. —Me encanta _____ suéter rosado. ¿Es nuevo?

2. —Sí, lo _____ hace dos días.

3. —¿Cuánto _____ por tu suéter?

4. —_____ veintiséis dólares.

5. —¡_____! ¿Por ese suéter tan bonito?

6. —Sí, sólo veintiséis dólares.

7. —Pues, es una _____ .

You are shopping in your favorite department store, but you have a very annoying salesperson waiting on you. The things that you are looking for are very different from what he is suggesting. First fill in the chart. Then, in order to complete the statements, describe each picture using the provided color. Follow the model.

Masculine singular	Feminine singular	Masculine plural	Feminine plural
rojo	roja	rojos	rojas
caro	_____	_____	_____
barato	_____	_____	_____
gris	_____	_____	_____
marrón	_____	_____	_____

—¿Qué desea, señora? *¿Una camisa roja?*

—No, busco *una camiseta azul.*

red　**blue**

1.

—¿Qué desea, señor? ¿_____ ?

—No, busco _____ .

gray　**black**

2.

—¿Qué desea, señorita? ¿_____ ?

—No, busco _____ .

green　**white**

3.

—¿Qué desea, señor? ¿_____ ?

—No, busco _____ .

brown　**yellow**

4.

—¿Qué desea, señor? ¿_____ ?

—No, busco _____ .

orange　**purple**

You and your dad are shopping together, but you can't seem to agree on anything. You like this and he likes that. Fill in the chart, then complete the statements with the correct demonstrative adjective. Follow the model.

Masculine singular	Feminine singular	Masculine plural	Feminine plural
este	_____	_____	_____
ese	_____	_____	_____

—¿Te gustan estos zapatos azules?

—No, prefiero *esos* zapatos rosados.

1. —¿Te gustan esos pantalones negros?

    —No, prefiero _____ pantalones azules.

2. —¿Te gusta esta falda?

    —No me gusta nada, pero me encanta _____ camisa.

3. —¿Te gustan esos tenis baratos?

    —Me gustan más _____ tenis caros.

4. —¿Te gusta ese vestido gris?

    —No, prefiero _____ vestido amarillo.

5. —¿Te gustan esas sudaderas baratas?

    —No, prefiero _____ sudaderas caras.

6. —¿Te gusta esa falda roja?

    —Sí, me gusta, pero me gusta más _____ falda azul.

7. —¿Te gustan esos jeans blancos?

    —No, prefiero _____ jeans negros.

8. —¿Te gusta este suéter marrón?

    —No, me gusta más _____ suéter blanco.

9. —¿Te gustan estas camisetas anaranjadas?

    —No, prefiero _____ camisetas grises.

10. —¿Te gusta este suéter rojo?

    —Pues, me gusta más _____ suéter rosado.

CAPÍTULO 6   Fecha

You have been shopping for weeks with no luck! Today, you finally find *some* clothes that look good on you and fit you well. Fill in the chart, then complete the statements with the correct direct object pronoun. Follow the model.

Masculine singular	Feminine singular	Masculine plural	Feminine plural
lo	_____	_____	_____

—¿Cómo te quedan esos zapatos?

—Me quedan bien. *Los* voy a comprar.

1. —¿Cómo te queda la camisa?

   —No me queda bien. No _____ compro.

2. —¿Cómo te quedan esas sudaderas?

   —No me quedan bien. No _____ voy a comprar.

3. —¿Cómo te queda ese vestido?

   —Me queda bien. _____ voy a comprar.

4. —¿Cómo te quedan estos pantalones cortos?

   —Me quedan bien, pero no _____ puedo comprar. Son muy caros.

5. —¿Cómo te queda la chaqueta?

   —Me queda bien y es barata. _____ compro.

6. —¿Quieres comprar el suéter?

   —Me queda grande. No _____ quiero comprar.

7. —¿Cómo te quedan las camisetas?

   —Me quedan bien, pero no _____ necesito.

8. —¿Cómo te quedan esos jeans?

   —Me quedan pequeños. No _____ compro.

9. —¿Quieres comprar las blusas?

   —Sí, me quedan bien. _____ quiero comprar.

10. —¿Cómo te queda la falda?

    —Me queda bien. _____ compro.

Your friends are very impressed with your new clothes. They are asking you where you bought them so that they can look for something similar. Complete each dialogue by identifying the picture and writing the correct direct object pronoun. Complete the chart first. Follow the model.

Masculine singular	Feminine singular	Masculine plural	Feminine plural
lo			

nuevo

—¿Dónde compraste tu *camisa nueva*?

—*La* compré en el almacén Gómez.

1. **caro**

—¿Dónde compraste tus _____?

— _____ compré en la zapatería.

2. **verde**

—¿Dónde compraste tu _____?

— _____ compré en la tienda de ropa.

3. **gris**

—¿Dónde compraste tus _____?

— _____ compré en la tienda de descuentos.

4. **blanco**

—¿Dónde compraste tu _____?

— _____ compré en el almacén Medellín.

5. **negro**

—¿Dónde compraste tus _____?

— _____ compré en la zapatería.

6. **azul**

—¿Dónde compraste tu _____?

— _____ compré en la tienda Hernández.

Gramática en contexto / El complemento directo: Los pronombres

Paso a paso 1

Nombre

CAPÍTULO 6

Fecha

Practice Workbook
Organizer

I. Vocabulary

Words about when something happened

_____

_____

_____

_____

Words to talk about shopping

_____

_____

_____

_____

Articles of clothing

_____

_____

_____

_____

_____

_____

_____

Colors

_____

_____

_____

_____

_____

_____

_____

Places to shop

_____

_____

_____

_____

_____

_____

_____

II. Grammar

1. Rule for adjective placement: _____ .

2. Demonstrative adjectives:

Masculine singular   Feminine singular

_____   _____

_____   _____

Masculine plural   Feminine plural

_____   _____

_____   _____

3. Direct object pronouns:

Masculine singular   Feminine singular

_____   _____

Masculine plural   Feminine plural

_____   _____

4. Rule for using direct object pronouns: _____

_____ .

A Vacation time is approaching and you and your family are trying to decide what to do. Everyone has a different opinion about what they want to do. Complete each statement by underlining the word or words that correctly identify the picture. Follow the model.

—¿Qué quieres hacer en las vacaciones, mamá?

—Quiero (tomar el sol / <u>sacar fotos</u>) de los lugares de interés.

1. —¿Qué quieres hacer en las vacaciones, abuelita?

—Quisiera (subir una pirámide / descansar) en México.

2. —Tomás, ¿qué prefieres hacer en las vacaciones?

—Prefiero (esquiar / bucear) en las montañas.

3. —Papá, ¿qué quieres hacer en las vacaciones?

—Quiero (descansar / bucear) en el mar.

4. —¿Qué quieres hacer en las vacaciones, Ana?

—Quisiera (practicar deportes / pasear en bote) en el lago del parque del Retiro.

5. —¿Qué prefieres hacer en las vacaciones, abuelito?

—Prefiero (tomar el sol / esquiar) en la playa.

6. —¿Qué quieres hacer en las vacaciones, Miguel?

—Quiero visitar (el museo / la playa) del Prado en España.

B Now complete the following sentences by underlining the correct word or words.

1. —¿Cuándo vas de vacaciones, Luisa?

—(Fuiste / Fui) de vacaciones el mes pasado.

2. —¿Adónde vas de vacaciones, Esteban?

—No voy a (ninguna parte / los recuerdos).

A As the school year draws to a close, your classmates are taking turns talking about where they have gone on vacation. Complete each statement by identifying the picture. Follow the model.

—¿Adónde fuiste el verano pasado, Isabel?

—Fui *a la catedral* de Burgos.

1. —Ricardo, ¿adónde fuiste el verano pasado?

—Fui _____ incas en Perú.

2. —María, ¿adónde fuiste el verano pasado?

—Fui _____ en Canadá.

3. —¿Adónde fuiste el verano pasado, Paula?

—Fui _____ para descansar y tomar el sol.

4. —¿Adónde fuiste el verano pasado, Rosa?

—Fui _____ de Yucatán.

B Now complete the dialogue using the words from the word bank.

descansar	explorar	el año pasado	recuerdos	sacar fotos
ninguna parte		la ciudad	lugares de interés	

1. —¿Adónde fuiste en las vacaciones _____ ?

2. —No fui a _____, pero este año quisiera visitar unos

_____ en _____ de San José en Costa Rica.

3. —¿Vas a comprar _____ ?

4. —¡Claro que sí! Y también voy a _____ .

5. —¿Vas a _____ la selva tropical de Costa Rica?

6. —No, prefiero _____ en las vacaciones.

You would like to go on a vacation with your friend Marisa, but neither one of you knows what the weather will be like where you are going. Complete each sentence by underlining the words that identify the picture. Follow the model.

—¿Qué tiempo hace en San Juan?

—Creo que (<u>hace calor</u> / hace frío).

1.

—¿Qué debo llevar si hace calor?

—Debes llevar (el traje de baño / el abrigo).

2.

—En esa ciudad siempre hace sol.

—¿Debo llevar (el impermeable / los anteojos de sol)?

3.

—¡Claro que sí! ¿Piensas ir a la playa?

—Sí, voy a llevar (el bronceador / el paraguas).

4.

—¿Qué otra cosa vas a llevar en (la maleta / la carpeta)?

5.

—Necesito llevar (una bufanda / un paraguas).

A Weather conditions have been unusual all across the country. When you turn on the weather station, reporters in different cities are commenting on the conditions and how they are coping. Write what they are saying according to the pictures. Follow the model.

Hace frío.

Menos mal que tengo *un abrigo.*

1. _____ .

   Menos mal que tengo _____ .

2. _____ .

   Menos mal que tengo _____ .

3. _____ .

   Menos mal que tengo _____ .

4. _____ .

   Menos mal que tengo _____ .

5. _____ .

   Menos mal que tengo _____ .

B Now complete the statements using the words in the word bank.

pasaporte	regresar	qué tiempo hace	salir	llevar

1. —¿ _____ en Costa Rica?

   —Creo que siempre hace sol.

2. —¿Cuándo piensas ir a Costa Rica?

   —Pienso _____ el primero de abril

   y _____ el quince de mayo.

3. —¿Qué piensas _____ contigo?

   —Una cámara, mi _____ y el bronceador.

Paso a paso 1   Nombre _____

CAPÍTULO 7   Fecha _____   Practice Workbook **7-5**

The weekend is finally here and there are many things you can't wait to do. Unfortunately, most of your friends have other plans or aren't prepared for the activities you want to do. They do suggest alternatives, however. Fill in the verb chart. Then complete each statement using the correct form of the verb *poder*.

Poder

yo	*pued-*_____	nosotros nosotras	*pod-*_____
tú	*pued-*_____	vosotros vosotras	podéis
Ud. él ella	*pued-*_____	Uds. ellos ellas	*pued-*_____

1. —¿_____ tú ir a la playa conmigo?

   —No, yo no _____. No tengo mis anteojos de sol.

   Pero nosotros _____ ir al museo. Ana quiere ir y ella

   _____ llevar una cámara.

2. —¿_____ ustedes ir a las montañas para

   esquiar con nosotros?

   —Juan y Elena _____, pero yo no _____. No tengo un abrigo.

   —Pues, nosotros _____ ir a la ciudad para explorar los

   lugares de interés.

3. —¿_____ José y María visitar el museo conmigo?

   —José quiere ir contigo, pero él no _____. Pero María sí _____

   y después Uds. _____ ir a la catedral.

4. —¿_____ Ud. ir al parque con nosotros?

   —No, yo no _____ ir con Uds. hoy. Pero nosotros _____ ir el

   domingo. También nosotros _____ pasear en bote.

CAPÍTULO 7

Your parents have gone away for the weekend and they left you in charge of your inquisitive little brother. You bring him along while you and your friends do errands and go through your weekend routine. Complete each statement according to the pictures using the expression formed by *para + infinitivo*. Follow the models.

I. —¿Por qué compras una cámara?

—La compro *para sacar fotos.*

1. —¿Por qué va Pablo al gimnasio?

—Pablo va al gimnasio _____.

2. —¿Por qué Juan va a comprar verduras y pollo?

—Juan los necesita _____.

3. —¿Por qué llevas un traje de baño?

—Lo llevo _____.

4. —¿Por qué vas al centro comercial?

—Voy _____.

II.   —¿Por qué necesitas *el bronceador?*

—*Lo necesito para tomar el sol.*

5. —¿Por qué necesita tu hermana _____?

— _____.

6. —¿Por qué necesitan Uds. _____?

— _____.

Paso a paso 1

Nombre _____

CAPÍTULO 7

Fecha _____

Practice Workbook **7-7**

Everyone in your family sets aside a particular month for certain activities. On New Year's Eve, you each fill in a calendar for the coming year. Complete the verb chart. Then complete the dialogues by writing the correct form of the verb *querer* and by identifying the pictures. Follow the model.

Querer

yo	quier-_____	nosotros nosotras	quer-_____
tú	quier-_____	vosotros vosotras	queréis
Ud. él ella	quier-_____	Uds. ellos ellas	quier-_____

—¿Qué *quieres* tú hacer en julio?

—*Yo quiero tomar el sol en julio.*

1. 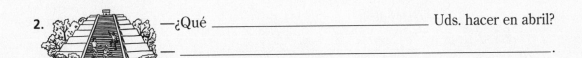 —¿Qué _____ Ud. hacer en enero?

— _____.

2. 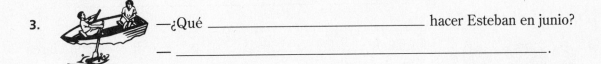 —¿Qué _____ Uds. hacer en abril?

— _____.

3.  —¿Qué _____ hacer Esteban en junio?

— _____.

4.  —¿Qué _____ Gloria y Margarita hacer en marzo?

— _____.

5.  —¿Qué _____ tú y Roberto hacer en mayo?

— _____.

Gramática en contexto / El verbo querer   **79**

You and your friends have signed up as exchange students in different parts of the world. Your sponsor families have sent you schedules highlighting the activities planned for your first week. Fill in the chart first. Then complete the dialogue according to the pictures. Follow the model.

Pensar

yo	*piens-* _____	nosotros nosotras	*pens-* _____
tú	*piens-* _____	vosotros vosotras	pensáis
Ud. él ella	*piens-* _____	Uds. ellos ellas	*piens-* _____

—¿Adónde *piensas* ir el lunes?   —*Pienso ir a las montañas.*
—¿Para qué?   —*Para esquiar.*

1.

—¿Adónde _____ ir el lunes tú y José?

— _____ .

—¿Para qué?

— _____ .

2.

—¿Adónde _____ ir Alicia el miércoles?

— _____ .

—¿Para qué?

— _____ .

3.

—¿Adónde _____ ir el sábado Marco
y Anita?

— _____ .

—¿Para qué?

— _____ .

4.

—¿Adónde _____ Ud. ir el domingo?

— _____ .

—¿Para qué?

— _____ .

A Your class is going on a field trip to a nearby city. Because most of the students know the city so well, the teachers are allowing you to travel in groups and to do whatever strikes you as interesting. You are asking one another what you would like to do. Follow the model, using the *a personal* when it is appropriate.

—¿Qué deseas hacer, Pilar?

—Deseo visitar _____ el museo.

1. —¿Qué te gustaría hacer, Cristina?

   —Me gustaría visitar _____ mi abuela.

2. —¿Qué quieres hacer, Daniel?

   —Quiero buscar _____ los recuerdos.

3. —¿Qué puedes hacer, Benjamín?

   —Puedo explorar _____ la ciudad.

4. —¿Qué deseas hacer, Magdalena?

   —Deseo escuchar _____ la profesora.

5. —¿Qué te gustaría hacer, Pablo?

   —Me gustaría visitar _____ mis tíos.

6. —¿Qué piensas hacer, Lucía?

   —Pienso _____ sacar fotos de las cataratas.

B Now write complete answers to the questions following the model.

—¿Qué piensas hacer, Mateo? (visitar / mi hermana)

—*Pienso visitar a mi hermana.*

1. —¿Qué quieres hacer, César? (dibujar / los lugares de interés)

   — _____.

2. —¿Qué puedes hacer, Yolanda? (ayudar / el profesor)

   — _____.

3. —¿Qué piensas hacer, Julia? (comprar / esa sudadera roja)

   — _____.

4. —¿Qué deseas hacer, Jaime? (buscar / mi amigo José)

   — _____.

CAPÍTULO 7

You really want to do something fun this weekend but everyone has already made plans. First fill in the verb charts. Then complete each dialogue by writing the correct form of *querer* in the first blank, *poder* in the second, and *pensar* in the third. Follow the model.

Poder

yo	*pued-*_____	nosotros nosotras	*pod-* _____
tú	*pued-*_____	vosotros vosotras	podéis
Ud. él ella	*pued-* _____	Uds. ellos ellas	*pued-* _____

Querer

yo	*quier-*_____	nosotros nosotras	*quer-* _____
tú	*quier-*_____	vosotros vosotras	queréis
Ud. él ella	*quier-* _____	Uds. ellos ellas	*quier-* _____

Pensar

yo	*piens-*_____	nosotros nosotras	*pens-* _____
tú	*piens-*_____	vosotros vosotras	pensáis
Ud. él ella	*piens-* _____	Uds. ellos ellas	*piens-* _____

—¿*Quieres* esquiar conmigo?

—No, no *puedo. Pienso* descansar.

1. —¿ _____ Uds. hablar por teléfono conmigo?

   —No, no _____ . _____ tomar el sol.

2. —¿ _____ Eva ver la televisión conmigo?

   —No, no _____ . _____ patinar.

3. —¿ _____ Graciela y Luz nadar conmigo?

   —No, no _____ . _____ ir al cine.

4. —¿ _____ tú y Cecilia tocar la guitarra conmigo?

   —No, no _____ . _____ cocinar.

5. —Y tú, Carlos, ¿ _____ ir de compras conmigo?

   —No, no _____ . _____ nadar.

Nombre _____

CAPÍTULO 7

Fecha _____

I. Vocabulary

Places to visit   Items to take

_____

_____

_____

_____

_____

_____

Things to do   Weather expressions

_____

_____

_____

_____

_____

_____

_____

II. Grammar

1. Verb charts

Querer		Poder		Pensar	
S	P	S	P	S	P
_____	_____	_____	_____	_____	_____
_____	queréis	_____	podéis	_____	pensáis
_____	_____	_____	_____	_____	_____

2. *Poder* means "can" or "to be able," so *puedo* means "I can." *Querer* means

_____ . *Pensar* means _____ . *Poder,*

querer and *pensar* are often followed by infinitives.

3. When do we use the *a personal?* _____

_____ .

4. When do we use *para + infinitivo?* _____

_____ .

After months of planning, your foreign exchange program has begun. Once you arrive at the home where you will be staying, you are so excited that you can't stop asking questions. To make things worse, you have misplaced most of your things! Complete each statement by underlining the words that correspond to the pictures. Follow the model.

—¿Dónde está mi camisa?

—Está en (<u>el dormitorio</u> / la cocina).

1.

—¿Dónde están mis cuadernos?

—Están en (el baño / la sala).

2.

—¿En qué cuarto de la casa puedo ver la televisión?

—La puedes ver en (la sala de estar / el comedor).

3.

—¿Dónde está tu abuelo?

—Está en (el garaje / el sótano).

4.

—¿Qué quehaceres debes hacer en tu casa?

—Tengo que (lavar la ropa / hacer la cama).

5.

—¿En qué cuarto de la casa comes?

—Como en (el coche / el comedor).

6.

—¿Qué quehaceres tienes que hacer hoy?

—Tengo que (arreglar el cuarto / sacudir los muebles).

7.

—¿Qué tengo que hacer?

—Tienes que (poner la mesa / quitar la mesa).

8.

—¿Qué más tienes que hacer hoy?

—Tengo que (cortar el césped / sacar la basura).

A You are staying with a friend for the weekend. Since you are in unfamiliar surroundings, your belongings are not where you are accustomed to finding them. Complete the dialogues according to the pictures. Follow the model.

—¿Dónde están mis *zapatos?*

—Creo que están en *el dormitorio.*

1.
—¿Dónde está mi _____?

—Creo que está en _____.

2.
—¿Dónde está mi _____?

—Creo que está en _____.

3.
—¿Dónde están mis _____?

—Creo que están en _____.

4.
—¿Dónde están las _____?

—Creo que están en _____.

5.
—¿Dónde está mi _____?

—Creo que está en _____.

B Continue your conversation with your friend. Complete these sentences by choosing words from the word bank.

más	cerca de	quehaceres	nuestro	tengo que	bastante

1. —¿Vives _____ la escuela?

   —No, vivo _____ lejos.

2. —¿Qué _____ tienes que hacer en tu casa?

   — _____ lavar los platos.

3. —¿Qué _____ tienen Uds. que hacer?

   —Pues, mi hermano y yo tenemos que arreglar _____ dormitorio.

A Along with your brothers and sisters, you are having an anniversary party for your parents, so you need to rearrange the whole house to accommodate the guests. Complete each sentence by underlining the correct word according to the pictures. Follow the model.

  —¿Dónde pones (<u>el equipo de sonido</u> / el cuadro)?

—Lo pongo cerca de (la ventana / <u>la videocasetera</u>).

1.   —¿Dónde ponen Uds. (la estufa / la mesa)?

—La ponemos cerca del (refrigerador / espejo).

2.   —¿Dónde ponen (la lámpara / la ventana)?

—La ponen cerca del (guardarropa / cartel).

3.   —¿Dónde pones (el escritorio / el sillón)?

—Lo pongo cerca del (sofá / cuadro).

4. —¿Dónde pones (los carteles / los coches)?

—Los pongo cerca de (la puerta / la ventana).

5.  —¿Dónde ponen Uds. (la cómoda / la cama)?

—La ponemos cerca del (escritorio / espejo).

B Your two cousins, who always disagree with each other, are helping you prepare for the party. Complete their statements by underlining the opposite of what is expressed.

1. —¡La ventana está sucia!
   —¿Sucia? ¡Está (limpia / redonda)!

2. —¡Esta silla es incómoda!
   —¿Incómoda? ¡Es (moderna / cómoda)!

3. —Me gusta ese espejo redondo. ¿Y a ti?
   —Prefiero este espejo (cuadrado / de cuero).

4. —No me gusta este sillón. Es muy antiguo.
   —Yo creo que es (de madera / moderno).

You and your family have just moved into a new apartment and you can't decide how to arrange things. Fortunately, your friends are there to help. Complete the conversations by writing in the words that correspond to the pictures. Follow the model.

—¿Dónde debo poner *el espejo*?

—Lo debes poner cerca *del sofá*.

1.

—¿Dónde debo poner _____ ?

—Lo debes poner cerca _____ .

2.

—¿Dónde debo poner _____ ?

—La debes poner cerca _____ .

3.

—¿Dónde debo poner _____ ?

—Lo debes poner cerca _____ .

4.

—¿Dónde debo poner _____ ?

—La debes poner cerca _____ .

5.

—¿Dónde debo poner _____ ?

—Lo debes poner cerca _____ .

6.

—¿Dónde debo poner _____ ?

—Lo debes poner cerca _____ .

7.

—¿Dónde debo poner _____ ?

—Lo debes poner cerca _____ .

8.

—¿Dónde debo poner _____ ?

—La debes poner cerca _____ .

A You and your family are such good cooks that people often call you for ideas (or for an invitation!). Complete the verb chart and then finish the sentences in **A** with the correct form of *hacer*.

Hacer

yo	*hag-* _____	nosotros nosotras	*hac-* _____
tú	*hac-* _____	vosotros vosotras	hacéis
Ud. él ella	*hac-* _____	Uds. ellos ellas	*hac-* _____

Poner

yo	*pong-* _____	nosotros nosotras	*pon-* _____
tú	*pon-* _____	vosotros vosotras	ponéis
Ud. él ella	*pon-* _____	Uds. ellos ellas	*pon-* _____

1. —¿Qué _____ tú para el desayuno?

—Yo _____ huevos y jamón.

2. —¿Qué _____ Uds. para la cena?

—Nosotros _____ arroz con pollo.

3. —¿Qué _____ tu hermano para el almuerzo?

—Él _____ una ensalada de tomates.

4. —¿Qué _____ tú y tu hermana para el almuerzo?

—Nosotros _____ una sopa de pollo.

B In addition to being good cooks your family is also very organized: everybody knows exactly where everything is. Review the verb chart above, then complete the dialogues with the correct form of *poner*.

1. —¿Dónde _____ tú el bistec?

—Yo lo _____ en el refrigerador.

2. —¿Dónde _____ Uds. las manzanas?

—Nosotros las _____ cerca de las naranjas.

3. —¿Dónde _____ el café tus padres?

—Lo _____ cerca del té.

4. —¿Dónde _____ Ana la guitarra?

—Ella la _____ en su dormitorio.

A The Peruvian exchange students are very anxious to explore your city. They are very disoriented, however. First complete the verb chart. Then finish the sentences with the correct form of *vivir*.

Vivir

yo	*viv-* _____	nosotros nosotras	*viv-* _____
tú	*viv-* _____	vosotros vosotras	vivís
Ud. él ella	*viv-* _____	Uds. ellos ellas	*viv-* _____

1. —María, ¿ _____ Ud. lejos del parque?

   —No, yo _____ cerca del parque.

2. —David, ¿ _____ Uds. en una casa?

   —No, nosotros _____ en un apartamento.

3. —Rosa, ¿ _____ tus primos cerca del almacén?

   —No, ellos _____ cerca del parque.

4. —Claudia, ¿ _____ tu abuelo cerca del museo?

   —No, él _____ cerca de la catedral.

5. —Pepe, ¿ _____ tú en el segundo piso?

   —No, yo _____ en el primer piso.

6. —Paco, ¿ _____ Lucía lejos de aquí?

   —No, ella _____ cerca de aquí.

7. —Cristina, ¿ _____ Eva y Felipe en el campo?

   —No, ellos _____ en la ciudad.

B Now that you know the endings to *-ar, -er,* and *-ir* verbs, complete the charts below by filling in the proper verb endings.

-ar		-er		-ir	
S	P	S	P	S	P
_____	_____	_____	_____	_____	_____
_____ -áis		_____ -éis		_____ -ís	
_____	_____	_____	_____	_____	_____

A Your polite cousins never directly reject your plans; rather, they state what they would prefer to do. First fill in the chart. Then complete the dialogues by writing in the correct forms of the verbs *querer* and *preferir*. Follow the model.

Preferir

yo	pref-_____	nosotros nosotras	pref-_____
tú	pref-_____	vosotros vosotras	preferís
Ud. él ella	pref-_____	Uds. ellos ellas	pref-_____

—¿*Quieren* Uds. ir al cine?

—Nosotros *preferimos* ir al centro.

1. —¿ _____ tú pasear en bote?

   —Yo _____ bucear.

2. —¿ _____ ellos nadar?

   —Ellos _____ escuchar música.

3. —¿Anita _____ ir al parque?

   —Ella _____ jugar videojuegos.

4. —¿ _____ Ud. visitar el museo?

   —Yo _____ descansar un poco.

5. —¿Tú y tu hermano _____ ir de pesca?

   —Nosotros _____ jugar vóleibol.

6. —¿ _____ Ramón subir una pirámide?

   —Él _____ explorar la selva.

B You have learned many other stem-changing verbs. Complete the charts below with the correct forms of these verbs.

Pensar		Poder	
S	P	S	P
_____	_____	_____	_____
_____	pensáis	_____	podéis
_____	_____	_____	_____

A Your older sister has just moved into a new apartment and your mother is asking about the furniture and other items she gave her. Complete the dialogues using the correct possessive adjective. Follow the model.

Possessive adjectives					
mi(s)	tu(s)	su(s)	nuestro(s), -a(s)	vuestro(s), -a(s)	su(s)

—¿Dónde está nuestro sillón?

—*Su / nuestro* sillón está en la sala.

1. —¿Dónde está mi mesa?

— _____ mesa está en la cocina.

2. —¿Dónde está nuestra videocasetera?

— _____ videocasetera está en la sala de estar.

3. —¿Dónde están sus cuadros?

— _____ cuadros están en el dormitorio.

4. —¿Dónde están tus carteles?

— _____ carteles están en el comedor.

B Your relatives have also generously donated their old furniture for your sister's new apartment. Write sentences showing ownership by naming the object in the picture and using the correct possessive adjective. Follow the model.

Es *el escritorio* de mi primo.

Es su escritorio.

1. Son _____ de mis abuelos.
   _____ .

2. Es _____ de mi hermana y yo.
   _____ .

3. Son _____ de mis padres y yo.
   _____ .

4. Son _____ de mi hermano y yo.
   _____ .

Each of your friends has a list of chores to do around the house. Choose the verb that best completes their dialogue. Make sure to use the correct form. If necessary, review the six forms of each verb in your other practice sheets. Follow the model.

—¿Qué *tienes* (poner / tener) que hacer en tu casa hoy?

—Yo *tengo* que limpiar el baño.

1. —Miguel, ¿ _____ (poner / hacer) tu coche en el garaje por la noche?

   —Sí, yo _____ mi coche en el garaje después de la cena.

2. —Rosa y Ricardo, ¿ _____ (preferir / vivir) Uds. pasar la aspiradora o lavar los platos?

   —Nosotros _____ lavar los platos.

3. —Sara, ¿ _____ (hacer / poner) tu hermana todos los quehaceres en tu casa?

   —Mi hermana _____ muchos quehaceres en nuestra casa.

4. —Pablo, ¿ _____ (hacer / vivir) tú en una casa de dos pisos?

   —Sí, yo _____ en una casa de dos pisos y tengo que hacer los quehaceres hoy.

5. —Ana, ¿nosotros _____ (poner / tener) que sacudir los muebles hoy?

   —Sí, Juan, ¡nosotros _____ que sacudir los muebles y sacar la basura hoy!

6. —Domingo, ¿ _____ (vivir / poner) tú y tu mamá en una casa con un lavadero?

   —Sí, mi mamá y yo _____ en una casa con un lavadero, pero yo _____ (tener / hacer) que lavar la ropa.

7. —¿Qué quehaceres _____ (poner / preferir) Ud. hacer?

   —Yo _____ arreglar mi cuarto.

8. —¿ _____ (poner / hacer) tú la mesa para tu familia todos los días?

   —No, yo no _____ la mesa. Mi prima y mi abuelito lo prefieren _____ (hacer / tener).

Paso a paso 1

Nombre _____

CAPÍTULO 8

Fecha _____

Practice Workbook
Organizer

I. Vocabulary

Rooms of houses	Household items	Descriptive words	Chores
_____	_____	_____	_____
_____	_____	_____	_____
_____	_____	_____	_____
_____	_____	_____	_____
_____	_____	_____	_____
_____	_____	_____	_____
_____	_____	_____	_____
_____	_____	_____	_____
_____	_____	_____	_____

II. Grammar

1. *Poner* and *hacer* are formed like regular *-er* verbs except for the *yo* forms,

   which are _____ and _____ .

2. The endings for regular *-ir* verbs are:

S	P
_____	_____
_____	-ís
_____	_____

3. When you want to say that you have to do something, you use this formula: _____

   _____ .

4. Possessive adjectives:

   _____   _____ o _____

   _____   vuestro(s)   o   vuestra(s)

   _____   _____

Paso a paso 1

CAPÍTULO 9

A The school nurse's office is very busy today. (Maybe everyone's trying to get out of taking the test they didn't study for!) Complete the dialogues by underlining the words that identify the picture. Follow the model.

  —¿Te duele (<u>la garganta</u> / la mano)?

—No, me duele (el cuello / <u>el estómago</u>).

1.   —¿Te duele (el pie / la cabeza)?

—No, me duele (la pierna / el dedo).

2.   —¿Te duele (el oído / la espalda)?

—No, me duele (el brazo derecho / la nariz).

3.   —¿Te duele (la mano / el cuello)?

—No, me duele (la espalda / la nariz).

4.   —¿Te duele (el dedo del pie / la mano)?

—No, me duele (la pierna / el pie).

5.   —¿Te duele (el ojo / la boca)?

—No, me duele (la pierna / la cabeza).

6.   —¿Te duele (el brazo / el pie)?

—No, me duele (el brazo / la mano).

B Now underline the best choice to complete these questions that the nurse might ask you.

1. —¿(Qué pasa / Cuánto tiempo hace que) te duele la mano?

—(Tengo / Hace) tres días.

2. —¡Ay! (No me siento bien / No me siento mal).

—Debes (llamar / doler) a tu médico.

3. —Debes (quedar bien / quedarte en cama) este fin de semana.

—Pues, creo que (no me duele nada / a ti te duele).

4. —¿Qué pasa? ¿Qué (me duele / te duele)?

—(Te duele / Me duele) el ojo izquierdo.

You are helping your three-year-old sister understand the relationship between various activities and the part of the body needed to perform them. Complete each statement according to the picture. Follow the model.

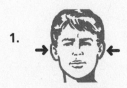

—¿Qué necesitas para jugar fútbol?

—*Necesito los pies.*

1. —¿Qué necesitas para escuchar música?

— _____ .

2. —¿Qué necesitas para hablar por teléfono?

— _____ .

3. —¿Qué necesitas para leer?

— _____ .

4. —¿Qué necesitas para patinar?

— _____ .

5. —¿Qué necesitas para nadar?

— _____ .

6. —¿Qué necesitas para jugar básquetbol?

— _____ .

7. —¿Qué necesitas para tocar la guitarra?

— _____ .

8. —¿Qué necesitas para estudiar?

— _____ .

On your way out the door, you overhear a telephone conversation between your mother and your older brother, who is away at college. Apparently, he isn't feeling very well. Complete the conversation by underlining the word or words that identify the picture. Follow the model.

—¿Por qué no puedes dormir?

—Porque tengo dolor de (garganta / <u>estómago</u>).

1.

—¿Por qué vas (a la clínica / al cine)?

—Porque tengo dolor de (oído / cabeza).

2.

—¿Por qué vas a (la enfermería / la dentista)?

—Porque tengo dolor de (garganta / muelas).

3.

—¿Por qué no puedes estudiar?

—Porque tengo (frío / un resfriado).

4.

—¿Qué tienes?

—Tengo (calor / gripe).

5.

—¿Por qué te sientes mal?

—Porque tengo (fiebre / dolor de cabeza).

6.

—¿Por qué no puedes leer?

—Porque tengo (calor / sueño).

7.

—¿Por qué no puedes ir a las clases?

—Porque tengo dolor de (muelas / garganta).

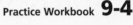

CAPÍTULO 9

A Many students have come to the clinic today. The nurse is asking each one the reason for his or her visit. Write their conversations according to the pictures. Follow the model.

— ¿Tienes *sueño?*

— *No, no tengo sueño. Tengo un resfriado.*

1. — ¿Tienes _____ ?

   — _____ .

2. — ¿Tienes _____ ?

   — _____ .

3. — ¿Tienes _____ ?

   — _____ .

4. — ¿Tienes _____ ?

   — _____ .

5. — ¿Tienes _____ ?

   — _____ .

B Now complete these conversations between the nurse and the students, using the words in the word bank.

cómo te sientes	tomar	peor	me lastimé

1. —¿Está mejor tu garganta?

   —No, está _____ . Debo quedarme en la cama.

2. —¿Por qué no vas a hacer ejercicio el viernes?

   —Porque _____ la pierna.

3. —¿ _____ ? ¿Todavía tienes fiebre?

   —No, ahora tengo sed.

During her nightly rounds, the doctor is asking the nurse how well her patients are sleeping. Fill in the verb chart. Then complete each dialogue by using the correct form of the verb *dormir* and by identifying the picture. Follow the model.

Dormir

yo	duerm-_____	nosotros nosotras	dorm-_____
tú	duerm-_____	vosotros vosotras	dormís
Ud. él ella	duerm-_____	Uds. ellos ellas	duerm-_____

—¿Cómo *duerme* Roberto?

—Roberto *duerme* mal porque *tiene frío.*

 1.

—¿Cómo _____ Ana y Luisa?

—Ana y Luisa _____ mal porque _____ .

 2.

—¿Cómo _____ tú?

—Yo _____ mal porque _____ .

 3.

—¿Cómo _____ Uds.?

—Nosotros _____ mal porque _____ .

 4.

—¿Cómo _____ Rosa?

—Ella _____ mal porque _____ .

 5.

—¿Cómo _____ Ud., señor Pérez?

—Yo _____ mal porque _____ .

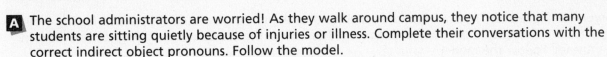

A The school administrators are worried! As they walk around campus, they notice that many students are sitting quietly because of injuries or illness. Complete their conversations with the correct indirect object pronouns. Follow the model.

Indirect object pronouns		
me	te	le

—¿Por qué no patina Héctor?

—Porque *le* duele la pierna.

1. —¿Por qué no comes?

   —Porque _____ duele el estómago.

2. —¿Por qué no estudia Margarita?

   —Porque _____ duele la cabeza.

3. —¿Por qué no hace Ud. ejercicio, señor?

   —Porque _____ duele la espalda.

4. —¡Ay! Profesor Martí, no me siento bien.

   —¿Qué _____ duele a ti?

5. —¿Cómo _____ sientes tú, Alberto?

   —Pues, _____ lastimé el dedo y no puedo jugar.

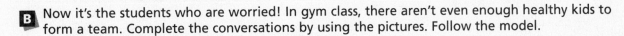

B Now it's the students who are worried! In gym class, there aren't even enough healthy kids to form a team. Complete the conversations by using the pictures. Follow the model.

—¿Te gustaría jugar con nosotros?

—*No puedo. Me duele la pierna.*

1. 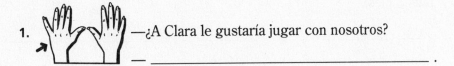 —¿A Clara le gustaría jugar con nosotros?

   — _____ .

2. 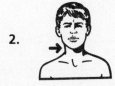 —Me gustaría jugar con Uds., pero _____ .

Everyone is depressed. They can't do the activities they enjoy most because they aren't feeling well. Complete the chart of indirect object pronouns. Then write the dialogues according to the words in parentheses. Follow the model.

Indirect object pronouns		
yo= _____	tú= _____	él, ella, Ud.= _____

(nadar / Ángel / pierna)

—¿*Le gusta nadar a Ángel?*

—*Sí, le encanta pero no puede. Le duele la pierna.*

(patinar / tú / espalda)

1. —¿ _____ ?

  — _____ .

(leer / Gloria / ojos)

2. —¿ _____ ?

  — _____ .

(hablar por teléfono / Pepe / garganta)

3. —¿ _____ ?

  — _____ .

(escuchar música / Ud. / oídos)

4. —¿ _____ ?

  — _____ .

(ayudar en casa / Julia / pies)

5. —¿ _____ ?

  — _____ .

(jugar videojuegos / tú / brazo)

6. —¿ _____ ?

  — _____ .

One of the reporters for the school newspaper is interviewing students to see how long they've been involved in certain activities. Complete the conversations according to the pictures and the information given. Follow the model.

¿**Cuánto tiempo hace que** + verb + subject?

Hace + time + **que** + present tense of the verb.

Pilar
6 years

—¿*Cuánto tiempo hace que nada Pilar?*

—*Hace seis años que nada.*

1. Sofía y Raquel
    9 months

—¿ _____ ?

— _____ .

2. tú
    10 years

—¿ _____ ?

— _____ .

3. Uds.
    7 weeks

—¿ _____ ?

— _____ .

4. Leonor
    13 years

—¿ _____ ?

— _____ .

5. los gemelos
    14 days

—¿ _____ ?

— _____ .

6. tu abuelo
    3 hours

—¿ _____ ?

— _____ .

Paso a paso 1 Nombre

CAPÍTULO 9 Fecha

Your best friend is very confused today, and you have to set him straight on everything. Complete each dialogue by using the information in parentheses. Follow the model.

—¿Miras la camisa azul? (rojo)

—*No, miro la roja.*

1. —¿Vas a comprar el cuaderno grande? (pequeño)

   — _____ .

2. —¿Hablas por teléfono con la muchacha alta? (bajo)

   — _____ .

3. —¿Te duele el brazo derecho? (izquierdo)

   — _____ .

4. —¿Compras los zapatos negros? (blancos)

   — _____ .

5. —Español es la segunda clase, ¿no? (primera)

   — _____ .

6. —¿Vas al cine con tu amiga perezosa? (trabajador)

   — _____ .

7. —¿Patinas con las muchachas prudentes? (atrevido)

   — _____ .

8. —¿Prefieres los zapatos nuevos? (viejos)

   — _____ .

9. —¿Te duele la mano izquierda? (derecho)

   — _____ .

10. —¿Te queda bien la falda morada? (rosado)

    — _____ .

Paso a paso 1

Nombre _____

CAPÍTULO 9

Fecha _____

**Practice Workbook
Organizer**

I. Vocabulary

Parts of the body

_____ _____ _____

_____ _____ _____

_____ _____ _____

_____ _____ _____

Words to ask and describe how someone is feeling

_____ _____

_____ _____

_____ _____

_____ _____

Words to use when talking about health

_____ _____

_____ _____

_____ _____

_____ _____

II. Grammar

1. The verb *to sleep:* _____

    S   P

_____ _____

_____ dormís

_____ _____

2. Indirect object pronouns: _____ ,

_____ , _____ .

3. To ask how long something has been going on, you use:

_____ + present tense of the verb.

To tell how long something has been going on, you use:

_____ + time + _____ + present tense of the verb.

4. Rule for dropping the noun: Avoid repeating the noun by using the definite or indefinite article with the adjective. Be sure that the adjective agrees with the noun it is replacing.

CAPÍTULO 10   Fecha _____

Your older brother just got his driver's license and he is offering to do errands for everyone! Your parents think he's just looking for an excuse to drive. Complete the conversations he has with your parents by underlining the words that identify the picture. Follow the model.

—¿A qué hora abre (<u>el banco</u> / el sello)?

—A las nueve. ¿Por qué?

—Tengo que (ir a pasear / <u>depositar dinero</u>).

1.

—¿Por qué vas a (la librería / la biblioteca)?

—Voy a (enviar una carta / devolver un libro).

2.

—Necesito comprar (sellos / comestibles). ¿Adónde debo ir?

—En (el supermercado / el correo) los tienen.

3.

—Yo vi (el dinero / el regalo) cerca de la puerta en (la farmacia / la tienda de regalos).

—¡Bueno! ¡Lo vamos a comprar!

4.

—(El dinero / El correo) va a abrir a las ocho. ¿Quisiera ir conmigo?

—Creo que sí. Tengo que (enviar una carta / sacar un libro).

5.

—¿Qué necesitas de (la tarjeta postal / la farmacia)?

—Tengo que comprar (pastillas para la garganta / la tarjeta de cumpleaños).

6.

—Me gustaría (ir a pasear / sacar un libro) hoy. ¿Y a ti?

—Yo prefiero (ver un partido de béisbol / enviar una carta).

A Your mother thinks you are very disorganized; she frequently tells you to do things you've already done! Read the first line of each conversation, then complete the second line with a word from the word bank. Follow the model.

vi	saqué	abrir	deposité	fui a pasear	hiciste	luego	envié

—¿Vas a devolver el libro hoy?

—No, ya lo *devolví* ayer.

1. —¿Vas a depositar dinero hoy?

   —No, ya lo _____ hace una hora.

2. —¿Vas a enviar el regalo hoy?

   —No, ya lo _____ anoche.

3. —¿Vas a pasear por la tarde?

   —No, ya _____ por la mañana.

4. —¿Vas a sacar un libro de la biblioteca?

   —No, ya lo _____ anoche.

5. —¿Vas a ver la tele ahora?

   —No, ya la _____ ayer.

B Your younger brother loves to contradict you. Complete each dialogue with the correct word from the word bank.

ayer	cerrar	temprano	doscientos	luego

1. —Siempre llegas tarde a la escuela.

   —No, siempre llego _____ .

2. —El correo va a abrir a las dos.

   —No, va a _____ a las dos.

3. —Tienes que comprar una tarjeta de cumpleaños hoy.

   —No, ya la compré _____ .

4. —Tengo cien sellos en mi colección.

   —No, tienes _____ .

The exchange students from Chile have arrived and are trying to orient themselves in your town. Complete the conversations below by underlining the word or words that identify the picture. Follow the model.

—¿Dónde queda (<u>el banco</u> / el correo)?

—Está entre (el supermercado / <u>la librería</u>) y la estación de servicio.

1.

—¿Dónde queda (la esquina / el hotel)?

—Está cerca del (teatro / estadio).

2.

—¿Dónde queda (la estación de servicio / la estación del tren)?

—Está lejos del templo, pero al lado del (correo / zoológico).

3.

—¿Dónde queda (la farmacia / el restaurante)?

—Está cerca de (la plaza / la esquina) Rivera.

4.

—¿Dónde queda (la estación de policía / la biblioteca)?

—Está a la izquierda (del taxi / de la estación del metro), cerca del correo.

5.

—¿Dónde queda (la tienda de regalos / la estación de servicio)?

—Está en (la avenida / la esquina) de Colón y Narváez.

6.

—¿Dónde queda (el teatro / el banco)?

—Está en la calle Prado, enfrente de (la estación del tren / la parada del autobús).

A Your cousins from the country have come to visit you in the city. Complete the conversations below by selecting and writing in the blank space the two appropriate words or groups of words. Follow the model.

en coche   —¿Cómo vamos a *la librería?*
a la librería
la esquina   —¡Ya sé! Podemos ir *en coche.*

1. el teatro   —¿Qué hay entre _____ y la tienda de regalos?
    a pie
    un restaurante   —Hay una farmacia y _____ .

2. a tres cuadras   —¿Qué hay cerca del _____ ?
    una estación de servicio
    hotel Plaza   —A ver... _____ .

3. avenida   —¿A cuántas cuadras queda la _____ Colón?
    al lado de
    dos cuadras   —Queda a _____ .

4. el taxi   —¿Dónde queda _____ ?
    entre
    la estación de policía   —Está _____ esta calle y la avenida Juárez.

5. el autobús   —¿Cómo piensas ir al _____ ?
    en taxi
    teatro   —Prefiero ir _____ .

6. detrás   —¿Está el estadio _____ de la plaza?
    en metro
    enfrente   —No, está _____ de la plaza.

B You've left your cousins to fend for themselves, and now they're lost. Complete the sentences by writing the opposite of the underlined word.

a la izquierda	enfrente de	al lado de	a pie

1. —¿Dónde queda la farmacia? ¿<u>Detrás de</u> la biblioteca?

    —No, la farmacia está _____ la biblioteca.

2. —¿Está la piscina <u>a la derecha</u> del supermercado?

    —No, la piscina está _____ del supermercado.

3. —¿Debemos ir <u>en autobús</u> a la plaza?

    —No, pueden ir _____ .

4. —¿Queda el cine <u>entre</u> el museo y el teatro?

    —No, el cine está _____ la biblioteca.

CAPÍTULO 10 Fecha

Practice Workbook **10-5**

Your city attracts many tourists, and they sometimes approach you for directions. Write conversations that correspond to the pictures. Follow the model.

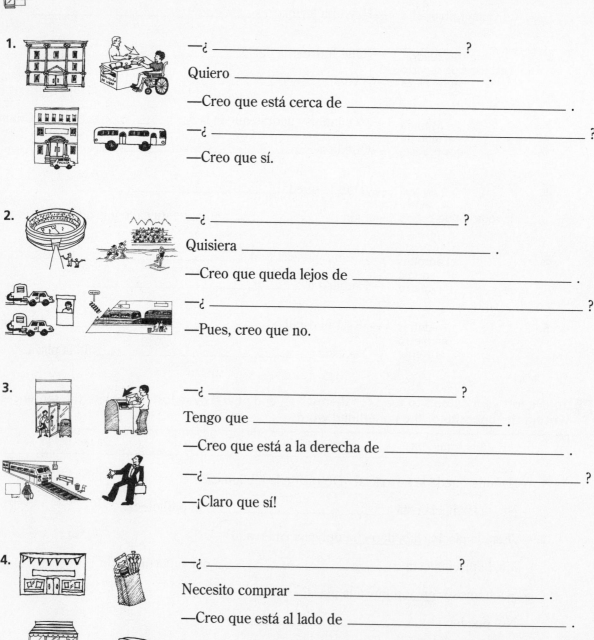

—*¿Dónde queda el banco?* Necesito *sacar dinero.*

—Creo que está al lado de *la farmacia.*

—*¿Puedo ir en coche?*

—Creo que sí.

1. —¿ _____ ?

Quiero _____ .

—Creo que está cerca de _____ .

—¿ _____ ?

—Creo que sí.

2. —¿ _____ ?

Quisiera _____ .

—Creo que queda lejos de _____ .

—¿ _____ ?

—Pues, creo que no.

3. —¿ _____ ?

Tengo que _____ .

—Creo que está a la derecha de _____ .

—¿ _____ ?

—¡Claro que sí!

4. —¿ _____ ?

Necesito comprar _____ .

—Creo que está al lado de _____ .

—¿ _____ ?

—Creo que sí.

You are visiting Spain and your sponsor family has agreed to let a group of you spend the day in Madrid. With several maps in hand, your group finds its way around the city. Complete the conversations according to the pictures and the accompanying word or words. Follow the model.

—¿Dónde está la farmacia?

—*Está cerca del hotel.*

1. a la
izquierda

—¿Dónde está el banco?

— _____ .

2. enfrente

—¿Dónde está el teatro?

— _____ .

3. entre

—¿Dónde está la biblioteca?

— _____ .

4. a la derecha

—¿Dónde está el zoológico?

— _____ .

5. lejos

—¿Dónde está la estación del metro?

— _____ .

6. al lado

—¿Dónde está la iglesia?

— _____ .

7. detrás

—¿Dónde está la farmacia?

— _____ .

Rule for using *del:* _____ .

Rule for using *al:* _____ .

Your mother calls home from work every day to check in on you and your siblings. First complete the verb chart. Then complete each dialogue using the preterite forms of the verbs in parentheses. Follow the model.

Preterite endings for -ar verbs

yo	_____	nosotros nosotras	_____
tú	_____	vosotros vosotras	-asteis
Ud. él ella	_____	Uds. ellos ellas	_____

(lavar / escuchar)

—Rosa, ¿*lavaste* tú los platos?

—No, yo *escuché* música.

(pasar / nadar)

1. —Carlos y David, ¿ _____ Uds. la aspiradora?

   —No, nosotros _____ .

(limpiar / patinar)

2. —¿ _____ el baño Ricardo?

   —No, Ricardo _____ .

(cocinar / hablar)

3. —¿ _____ el pollo tú y Alicia?

   —No, nosotras _____ por teléfono.

(cortar / tomar)

4. —¿ _____ el césped los gemelos?

   —No, ellos _____ el sol.

(arreglar / dibujar)

5. —¿ _____ tú el cuarto?

   —No, yo _____ .

Your cousin is thinking about vacationing in Venezuela. Since you traveled there last year, write her a letter about your experiences. First complete the verb chart. Then complete the letter by using the preterite forms of the verbs in the word bank.

Preterite endings for -ar verbs

yo	_____	nosotros nosotras	_____
tú	_____	vosotros vosotras	-asteis
Ud. él ella	_____	Uds. ellos ellas	_____

preguntar	regresar	buscar	pagar	sacar
practicar	escuchar	mirar	llegar	tocar
	caminar	enviar	visitar	

Estimada Carmela:

El año pasado mi hermana Eva y yo fuimos a Venezuela. Cuando nosotras ____1____ al hotel, yo ____2____ el champú, el jabón y la pasta dentífrica en la maleta. ¡Vaya! ¡Yo no sabía que mi hermana ____3____ esas cosas de la maleta. Fui a comprar más en la tienda del hotel. ¡Qué caro! Por eso fui a una farmacia y no ____4____ mucho. Después, Eva y yo ____5____ hasta la plaza con un monumento en el centro y muchas flores. Unos jóvenes ____6____ guitarras y Eva y yo ____7____ la música. Luego un muchacho guapo nos ____8____ :

"¿Tienen hambre? ¿Quieren comer conmigo y mis amigos?"

"Bueno, pero tenemos que ir ahora si queremos regresar temprano al hotel."

Luego fuimos al parque. El muchacho y sus amigos ____9____ deportes. Eva y yo ____10____ lugares de interés. Después, Eva ____11____ unas tarjetas postales en el correo.

Cuando Eva y yo ____12____ a nuestra casa, ____13____ las fotos que nos ____14____ nuestro amigo de Venezuela.

¡Qué vacaciones tan interesantes!

Rule for forming the *yo* form of *-car* and *-gar* verbs and stem-changing verbs:

_____

_____

Your geography class is compiling a travel log. The class is sharing information about where they've traveled. First complete the verb chart. Then complete the conversations using the words in parentheses and the correct preterite form of the verb *ir*. Follow the model.

Preterite tense of *ir*

yo	fu-_____	nosotros nosotras	fu-_____
tú	fu-_____	vosotros vosotras	fuisteis
Ud. él ella	fu-_____	Uds. ellos ellas	fu-_____

(Teresa / montañas) (Ana / ruinas)

—*Teresa fue a las montañas.*

—*Ana fue a las ruinas.*

(yo / museo) (Juana y Raúl / catedral)

1. — _____ .

   — _____ .

(nosotros / pirámides) (tú /mar)

2. — _____ .

   — _____ .

(Uds. / cataratas) (Ud. / selva tropical)

3. — _____ .

   — _____ .

(él / playa) (ella / zoológico)

4. — _____ .

   — _____ .

(Jaime y Tomás / campo) (Alonso y Clara / parque de diversiones)

5. — _____ .

   — _____ .

Paso a paso 1   Nombre _____

CAPÍTULO 10   Fecha _____

I. Vocabulary

Places

_____

_____

_____

_____

Errands and activities

_____

_____

_____

_____

Words to indicate location

_____

_____

_____

_____

Words to indicate when an event occurred

_____

_____

_____

_____

II. Grammar

1. The preposition *de* used with *el* forms the contraction *del*.

S	P
del	_____
_____	_____

2. Preterite endings of *-ar* verbs:

S	P
_____	_____
_____	-asteis
_____	_____

3. Preterite forms of the verb *ir:*

S	P
_____	_____
_____	fuisteis
_____	_____

Your sociology class is taking a survey to determine people's likes and dislikes in movies and television programs. Complete each sentence by underlining the words which best identify the picture. Follow the model.

—¿Qué piensas de (<u>los programas educativos</u> / los programas de entrevistas)?

—Pienso que son interesantes.

1.

—¿Qué clase de programa es?

—Son (los dibujos animados / las noticias).

2.

—¿Qué piensas de (la telenovela / el anuncio)?

—Es muy aburrida.

3.

—¿Qué clase de programa es?

—Es (un documental / un programa de detectives).

4.

—(Las comedias / Las noticias) son interesantes, ¿no?

—Sí, pero son tristes también.

5.

—¿Te interesa ver (el pronóstico del tiempo / las noticias)?

—Pues, a veces.

6.

—¿Qué clase de programa es?

—Es (un programa de entrevistas / un programa educativo).

Vocabulario para conversar

A You have only one TV in your house, and everyone wants to watch a different program. Complete each dialogue by identifying the picture. Follow the model.

—¿Qué clase de programa te interesa ver?

—Me interesa ver *un programa de detectives.*

1.

—¿Qué clase de programa te interesa ver?

—Me interesa ver _____ .

2.

—¿Qué clase de programa te interesa ver?

—Me interesa ver _____ .

3.

—¿Qué clase de programa te interesa ver?

—Me interesa ver _____ .

4.

—¿Qué clase de programa te interesa ver?

—Me interesa ver _____ .

B Now complete these dialogues using words from the word bank.

cómicas	me dan miedo	comedias	cuál	fascina

1. —¿Qué piensas de las _____ del canal 5?

2. —¡Me encantan! Son divertidas y _____ . Pero a veces
   _____ las noticias.

3. —¿ _____ es el programa más emocionante?

4. —A mí me _____ la telenovela de las ocho.

A You love movies, but you are always running late for the showings. You constantly have to ask your friends what movies are showing and at what times. Complete each dialogue by underlining the words that best identify the picture. Follow the model.

—¿A qué hora dan (la película de terror / <u>la película del oeste</u>)?

—A las cuatro en punto.

1.

—¿Cuándo empieza (la película de terror / la película musical)?

—Empieza en media hora.

2.

—¿Va a ser larga (la película de ciencia ficción / la película romántica)?

—No. Empieza a las dos y veinticinco, y termina a las tres y media.

3.

—¿Cuánto dura (la película de aventuras / la película musical)?

—Dura una hora y quince minutos.

4.

—¿Cuándo va a empezar (la película de terror / la película romántica)?

—Empieza a las tres menos cuarto.

5.

—Ya es la una y veinte. ¿Qué podemos hacer?

—Podemos ir al cine a ver (una película de aventuras / una película del oeste).

B Now complete the following conversation using words from the word bank.

de la tarde	hasta	puntualmente	solamente	larga

1. —Quiero ver la película que dan a las dos _____ .

2. —¿Es muy _____ ?

3. —No, _____ dura una hora y media.

4. —Bueno, vamos. Quiero llegar _____ .

A Your sister has just returned after spending three months in Colombia. Now she's eager to find out about the latest movies and TV programs. Circle the letter of the correct answer to her questions. Follow the model.

—¿Cuál es la mejor película de la semana?

    a. —Pues, podemos ir más tarde.

    (b.) —Yo pienso que es la película romántica "Amor de siempre."

1. —¿Te gustan las películas de terror?

    a. —No, no me gusta ese programa.

    b. —Pues, sí. ¡Me fascinan!

2. —¿Qué piensas de la película de ciencia ficción que dan en el cine Vox?

    a. —Creo que es muy larga. Dura tres horas.

    b. —Sí, empieza a las cinco en punto.

3. —¿Hasta qué hora de la noche dan esa película?

    a. —Creo que más temprano.

    b. —Creo que hasta las nueve en punto.

4. —Quiero ver la película de aventuras esta noche. ¿Quieres ir conmigo?

    a. —En media hora puedo ir contigo.

    b. —Todavía no. Es muy corta.

B Now complete these statements using words from the word bank.

casi	media hora	un poco	hasta

1. El concierto va a empezar en _____ . ¡Menos mal!

2. Las películas musicales me gustan _____ más que las

del oeste.

3. Son _____ las ocho. La película dura

_____ las ocho.

A You and your friend can never decide which movies or programs to watch together. Complete these dialogues using the pictures and the words given. Follow the model.

interesante

—Pienso que *un programa de detectives es más interesante que un programa de hechos de la vida real.* ¿Y tú?

—Pienso que *un programa de detectives es menos interesante que un programa de hechos de la vida real.*

1. emocionante

—Pienso que _____

_____ . ¿Y tú?

—Pienso que _____

_____ .

2. cómico

—Pienso que _____

_____ . ¿Y tú?

—Pienso que _____

_____ .

3. realista

—Pienso que _____

_____ . ¿Y tú?

—Pienso que _____

_____ .

B Now answer these questions by using the comparative form of the underlined words.

1. Rosa es <u>buena</u> estudiante. ¿Y Susana?

_____ .

2. Paco López es un actor <u>malo</u>. ¿Y Pablo Cortéz?

_____ .

3. La hermana de Raúl es joven. ¿Y la hermana de Sara?

_____ .

Paso a paso 1

Nombre _____

CAPÍTULO 11

Fecha _____ Practice Workbook **11-6**

Because there is an important project coming up, your teacher is trying to form pairs of people who have similar tastes. She is conducting a survey, asking people about their likes and dislikes in a variety of categories. Complete each dialogue according to the picture. Follow the model. (Think carefully about the irregular forms.)

la fruta / sabroso

—¿Cuál es *la fruta más sabrosa?*

—*La fruta más sabrosa es la manzana.*

1. **la ropa / caro**

—¿Cuál es _____

_____ ?

— _____

_____ .

2. **la clase / aburrido**

—¿Cuál es _____

_____ ?

— _____

_____ .

3. **el cuarto / desordenado**

—¿Cuál es _____

_____ ?

— _____

_____ .

4. **la bebida / bueno para la salud**

—¿Cuál es _____

_____ ?

— _____

_____ .

5. **la bebida / malo para la salud**

—¿Cuál es _____

_____ ?

— _____

_____ .

Gramática en contexto / Los superlativos **119**

Your mother thinks you do everything at the last possible minute. Sure enough, you still haven't completed any of the things that she asks you about. You are planning to do it all tomorrow! Complete each dialogue according to the picture. Follow the model.

—¿Compraste *una cámara ayer?*

—*No, pero voy a comprarla mañana.*

1. —¿Cocinaste _____ ayer?

— _____ .

2. —¿Lavaste _____ ayer?

— _____ .

3. —¿Enviaste _____ ayer?

— _____ .

4. —¿Viste _____ ayer?

— _____ .

5. —¿Arreglaste _____ ayer?

— _____ .

6. —¿Sacaste _____ de la biblioteca ayer?

— _____ .

7. —¿Viste _____ ayer?

— _____ .

8. —¿Compraste _____ ayer?

— _____ .

Gramática en contexto / El complemento directo: Los pronombres y el infinitivo

You were sick last night and you weren't able to go out. It seems as if everyone else did though, and you would like to know how their evening went. First fill in the verb chart. Then complete the dialogues with the correct form of the preterite of the verb *ver*. Follow the model.

Preterite of *ver*

yo	v- _____	nosotros nosotras	v- _____	
tú	v- _____	vosotros vosotras	visteis	
Ud. él ella	v- _____	Uds. ellos ellas	v- _____	

—¿*Viste* tú una película anoche?

—*Sí, yo la vi anoche.*

1. —¿ _____ Uds. el concierto anoche?

   — _____ .

2. —¿ _____ Luisa y Lourdes a su tía anoche?

   — _____ .

3. —¿ _____ el profesor de español a Carmela anoche?

   — _____ .

4. —¿ _____ Jaime y Pepe el programa de hechos de la vida real anoche?

   — _____ .

5. —¿ _____ tú los dibujos animados anoche?

   — _____ .

6. —¿ _____ Ud. mi nuevo coche anoche?

   — _____ .

7. —¿Vieron Uds. la comedia de Tomás anoche?

   — _____ .

8. —¿ _____ Elena mis fotos de las pirámides?

   — _____ .

You are taking care of your little sister for the day. She has questions about everything! Using the correct indirect object pronoun from the chart, complete the responses. Follow the model.

Indirect object pronouns

yo → me	nosotros / nosotras → nos
tú → te	vosotros / vosotras → os
él / ella / Ud. → le	ustedes / ellos / ellas → les

—¿Por qué come Federico ensalada?

—Pues, porque *le* gusta.

1. —¿Por qué no ven Uds. el programa musical?

   —Pues, porque no _____ interesa.

2. —¿Por qué estudian ciencias Miguel y Alicia?

   —Pues, porque _____ fascinan.

3. —¿Por qué visitas tú el museo?

   —Pues, porque _____ encanta.

4. —¿Por qué no ve la película de terror tu mamá?

   —Pues, porque _____ da miedo.

5. —¿Por qué no estudia inglés Guillermo?

   —Pues, porque no _____ interesa.

6. —¿Por qué cocinas tú huevos fritos?

   —Pues, porque _____ gustan.

7. —¿Por qué escuchan esa música tus padres?

   —Pues, porque _____ encanta.

8. —¿Por qué practican deportes Uds.?

   —Pues, porque _____ gustan.

Your friends are sleeping over at your house and you are trying to decide what to watch on TV. Write dialogues based on the pictures and words provided. Be sure to use the first choice to answer the first question. Follow the model.

emocionante

¿Qué quieres ver, una película de terror o un programa musical?

A mí me interesa la película de terror.

¿Por qué?

Porque pienso que una película de terror es más emocionante que un programa musical.

¡Vamos a verla!

divertido

1. _____
   _____
   _____
   _____

realista

2. _____
   _____
   _____
   _____

cómico

Enrique

3. _____
   _____
   _____
   _____

Paso a paso 1

Nombre

CAPÍTULO 11

Fecha

Practice Workbook
Organizer

I. Vocabulary

Types of movies and TV shows	Words to describe movies and shows	Words to indicate time or duration
___	___	___
___	___	___
___	___	___
___	___	___
___	___	___
___	___	___

II. Grammar

1. To compare two objects, use the formula _____ to say that one thing is *more* than another.

2. To compare two objects, use the formula _____ to say that one thing is *less* than another.

3. The four exceptions that do not use *más* are:

   bueno = _____   malo = _____

   viejo = _____   joven = _____

4. To say that someone or something is "the most" of a group, use the formula

   _____ .

5. When we use direct object pronouns with infinitives, we can either _____

   _____ .

6. Preterite of *ver:*

S	P
___	___
___	visteis
___	___

7. Indirect object pronouns:

S	P
___	___
___	os
___	___

Paso a paso 1   Nombre _____

 CAPÍTULO 12   Fecha _____   Practice Workbook **12-1**

A new Mexican restaurant has opened in town. Some of your friends have tried it, but others are eating there for the first time. Complete each dialogue by underlining the words that identify the picture or pictures. Follow the model.

—¿Qué vas a pedir de plato principal?

—Quisiera probar (las quesadillas / <u>los tacos</u>).

1.
—¿Has probado (el helado / los churros)?

—Sí, pero yo prefiero (los pasteles / el flan).

2.
—¿Qué plato vas a probar?

—Pienso probar (los frijoles refritos / los chiles rellenos).

3.
—¿Qué vas a pedir de plato principal?

—Quisiera probar (el chile con carne / las enchiladas).

4.
—¿Has probado (las salsas / el aguacate)?

—Sí, son picantes.

5.
—¿Has probado (los pasteles / los churros)?

—Sí, he probado (el chocolate / el flan) también.

6.
—¿Cuál es tu plato favorito?

—Me encantan (las enchiladas / los burritos).

7.
—¿Quieres probar (el guacamole / el chile)?

—Sí, voy a probarlo ahora mismo.

Vocabulario para conversar   **125**

Copyright © Scott, Foresman and Company

A Adriana loves to spend Sunday afternoons in the kitchen with her grandmother learning how to cook by observing and asking questions. Complete their dialogue according to the pictures. Follow the model.

—¿Con qué se hacen *los tacos?*

—Se hacen con *tortillas de maíz.*

1. —¿Con qué se hacen estas _____ ?

   —Se hacen con _____ y _____ .

2. —¿Con qué se hacen los burritos?

   —Se hacen con _____ y _____ .

3. —¿Con qué se hacen _____ ?

   —Se hacen con _____ y _____ .

4. —¿Con qué se hacen _____ ?

   —Se hacen con _____ y _____ .

B Now complete this conversation with your grandmother using the words from the word bank.

a menudo	el postre	picante	probarla	muchas veces

1. —¿Te gusta cocinar la comida _____ , abuelita?

   —Sí, y me gusta _____ también.

2. —¿Comes chiles rellenos _____ ?

   —Sí, _____ . Pero prefiero _____ después del plato principal.

You have just started your job as a waiter at a neighborhood restaurant. Complete the dialogues by underlining the words that best identify the pictures. Follow the model.

—Camarero, me falta (<u>un cuchillo</u> / la cuchara).

—Lo traigo en seguida.

1.

—Camarero, no tengo (un tazón / un tenedor).

—Está cerca de (la cuchara / la taza).

2.

—Camarero, ¿me trae (la servilleta / el menú), por favor?

—Está delante del (azúcar / platillo), señora.

3.

—Camarero, necesito (la sal / el plato) y (el vaso / la pimienta).

—En seguida las traigo, señor.

4.

—Camarero, ¿dónde está (la mantequilla / la cuenta)? No la veo.

—Aquí está, debajo de (la servilleta / el tazón).

5.

—Quiero café, pero no tengo ni (un vaso / una taza) ni
(un platillo / un cuchillo).

—En seguida los traigo, señor.

6.

—Camarero, ¿me trae (un tenedor / un plato)?

—Sí, voy a traerlo en seguida, y (un tazón / un tenedor) también.

7.

—Camarero, (la cuenta / la cuchara), por favor.

—Está al lado del (vaso / cuchillo), señorita.

A You have a large family and whenever you eat meals together everyone is constantly talking. Complete the dialogues by identifying the pictures. Follow the model.

—¿Me pasas *la sal,* por favor?

—Sí, aquí la tienes.

1. —¿Me pasas _____ , por favor?

—¡Claro que sí! ¿Necesitas _____ también?

—Ahora no, gracias.

2. —¿Me pasas _____ y _____ ?

—Sí, aquí las tienes.

3. —¿Necesitas _____ , abuelita?

—Ahora no, gracias. Pero sí necesito _____ .

4. —¿Me pasas _____ , por favor?

—Aquí la tienes, y _____ también.

B Now complete this dialogue using the words from the word bank.

lo mismo	especialidad de la casa	pediste	a la carta

1. —¿Qué _____ en el restaurante mexicano?

—Pues, pedí tacos de pollo _____ .

2. —Yo también pedí _____ . Creo que son la _____

_____ .

A For your grandfather's 80th birthday, your family has planned a gala celebration. The grandchildren are taking the guests' orders and serving the food. First fill in the verb chart. Then complete the conversations by using the correct form of the verb *pedir*. Follow the model.

	Pedir	**Servir**
yo	p- _____	s- _____
tú	p- _____	s- _____
él / ella / Ud.	p- _____	s- _____
nosotros / nosotras	p- _____	s- _____
vosotros / vosotras	pedís	servís
ellos / ellas / Uds.	p- _____	s- _____

—¿Qué *pide* Ud. de plato principal, Ana?

—Yo *pido* chile con carne, por favor.

1. —¿Qué _____ Uds. de plato principal, Felipe y Pepe?

   —Nosotros _____ las quesadillas.

2. —¿Qué _____ tus hermanas de postre, Carlos?

   —Mis hermanas _____ queso y fruta casi siempre.

3. —¿Qué _____ tú de plato principal, papá?

   —Yo _____ los chiles rellenos.

4. —¿Qué _____ su hijo de postre, Luis?

   —Mi hijo _____ flan.

5. —¿Qué _____ de plato principal Ricardo y tú?

   —Ricardo y yo _____ los tacos.

B Now it's time to serve the dinner! Use the correct form of the verb *servir*.

1. Pepe les _____ unos tacos sabrosos a Ricardo y a ti.

2. Mis primas nos _____ chiles rellenos.

3. Yo les _____ queso y fruta a tus hermanas.

4. Me encantan las quesadillas. Tú me las _____ en la cena.

5. Nosotros le _____ enchiladas a Ana.

A group of students is going to work on a school project. Each person must bring a different item that they will be needing. First fill in the verb chart. Then, using the correct form of the verb *traer*, complete each dialogue. Follow the model.

Traer

yo	tra- _____	nosotros nosotras	tra- _____
tú	tra- _____	vosotros vosotras	traéis
Ud. él ella	tra- _____	Uds. ellos ellas	tra- _____

—¿Quién trae los libros? **(Alicia)**

—*Alicia los trae.*

1. —¿Quién trae los marcadores? **(Raúl y Diego)**

    — _____ .

2. —¿Quién trae la calculadora? **(yo)**

    — _____ .

3. —¿Quién trae los lápices? **(tu hermana)**

    — _____ .

4. —¿Quién trae las reglas? **(nosotros)**

    — _____ .

5. —¿Quién trae la carpeta de argollas? **(tú)**

    — _____ .

6. —¿Quién trae los bolígrafos? **(sus primos)**

    — _____ .

A group of friends likes to get together in the spring for a potluck picnic. First complete the verb chart, then write the dialogues based on the pictures. Follow the model.

	Pedir	Traer	Servir
yo	_____	_____	_____
tú	_____	_____	_____
él / ella / Ud.	_____	_____	_____
nosotros / nosotras	_____	_____	_____
vosotros / vosotras	pedís	traéis	servís
ellos / ellas / Uds.	_____	_____	_____

Jaime y Beatriz yo
Lucía

—*Jaime y Beatriz piden chile con carne. Yo traigo pescado. ¿Qué sirve Lucía?*

—*Lucía sirve papas al horno.*

1.   **tú   Juana**   — _____

— _____ .

sus primos   — _____ .

2.   **yo   nosotros**   — _____

— _____ .

tú   — _____ .

3.   **Isabel y yo   tú**   — _____

— _____ .

Uds.   — _____ .

Some people deliver things early, and some wait until the next day to do it. First fill in the indirect object pronoun chart. Then complete the dialogues according to the pictures. As you do so, remember that the picture refers to the question. Follow the model. (Look carefully at the changes in the answer.)

Indirect object pronouns

Singular		Plural	
yo →	_____	nosotros / nosotras →	_____
tú →	_____	vosotros / vosotras →	os
él / ella / Ud. →	_____	ellos / ellas / Uds. →	_____

—¿Le trae el libro a ella hoy?

—*No, va a traerle (le va a traer) el libro mañana.*

1. —¿Me traes la cámara mañana?

—_____ .

2. —¿Les traemos los recuerdos (a ellos) hoy?

—_____ .

3. —¿Nos trae Luis Enrique las calculadoras hoy?

—_____ .

4. —¿Te traigo los anteojos de sol mañana?

—_____ .

5. —¿Le traen sus padres el pasaporte (a él) hoy?

—_____ .

6. —¿Les trae Maricruz el bronceador (a Uds.) mañana?

—_____ .

You missed last night's party, so you decide to call a friend to find out how it went. First fill in the verb chart. Then complete the dialogues using the correct preterite form of the most appropriate verb from the word bank. Follow the model.

Preterite endings of -er and -ir verbs

yo	_____	nosotros nosotras	_____
tú	_____	vosotros vosotras	isteis
Ud. él ella	_____	Uds. ellos ellas	_____

comer	salir	subir	vivir	abrir	beber

—¿Quiénes *comieron* hamburguesas y papas fritas?

—Rosa, Rigoberto y Carlos las *comieron*.

1. —¿Cuándo _____ Alejandro su regalo?

   —Él lo _____ a las diez y media, más o menos.

2. —¿A qué hora _____ tú de la fiesta?

   —Yo _____ a la medianoche.

3. —¿Quién _____ el refresco?

   —Emilia _____ el refresco y ella _____

   los tacos también.

4. —¿Cuándo _____ tú el regalo de tu tía?

   —Yo lo _____ cuando Cecilia _____ el regalo tuyo.

5. —¿Quién _____ los churros?

   —Teresa y yo los _____ y Manuel _____ el flan.

6. —¿A qué hora _____ Salvador?

   —Salvador _____ a las once y media, y tus primos

   _____ a las once y veinticinco.

7. —¿ _____ tú café o té?

   —Yo _____ té, pero Susana y Rosalinda _____ café.

Gramática en contexto / El pretérito de los verbos que terminan en -er e -ir **133**

Everybody in your family seems to be running a day late. With this in mind, complete the dialogues by using the words from the word bank. Fill in the verb chart first. Follow the model.

	Present tense of *-er* verbs	Present tense of *-ir* verbs	Preterite tense of *-er* and *-ir* verbs
yo	_____	_____	_____
tú	_____	_____	_____
él / ella / Ud.	_____	_____	_____
nosotros / nosotras	_____	_____	_____
vosotros / vosotras	-éis	-ís	-isteis
ellos / ellas / Uds.	_____	_____	_____

comer	salir	subir	vivir	abrir	beber

—¿*Come* Margarita un sandwich de jamón y queso hoy?

—*No, Margarita ya lo comió ayer.*

1. —¿ _____ tú café hoy en el almuerzo?

   — _____ .

2. —¿ _____ las ventanas Sara y Lupita hoy?

   — _____ .

3. —¿ _____ Uds. huevos en el desayuno hoy?

   — _____ .

4. —¿ _____ tú la carta de tía Anita hoy?

   — _____ .

5. —¿ _____ Uds. chocolate en la merienda hoy?

   — _____ .

6. —¿ _____ Catalina y Lorena del hospital hoy?

   — _____ .

Paso a paso 1

Nombre _____

CAPÍTULO 12

Fecha _____

Practice Workbook
Organizer

I. Vocabulary

Names of foods	Table settings	Words to talk about food

Words to indicate time	Words to indicate position

II. Grammar

1. Some *-ir* verbs change their stem from an _____ to an _____ in the *yo, tú, Ud., él, ella, Uds., ellos,* and *ellas* forms. *Pedir* and *servir* are two examples.

2.

Pedir		Servir		Traer	
S	P	S	P	S	P
_____	_____	_____	_____	_____	_____
_____	pedís	_____	servís	_____	traéis
_____	_____	_____	_____	_____	_____

3. An indirect object pronoun tells _____ or _____ an action is performed.

4. We can attach an indirect object pronoun to _____ or put it _____ .

5. Preterite endings of *-er* and *-ir* verbs:

S	P
_____	_____
_____	-isteis
_____	_____

You and your friends are trying to get everyone in school to recycle and save energy. Each time you see someone being careless with the environment, you rush over to them to explain your cause. Complete each dialogue by underlining the words that identify the picture. Follow the model.

—¿Qué vas a hacer con (<u>las latas</u> / las revistas)?

—Voy a reciclarlas.

1.

—¿Qué piensas hacer con (los plásticos / los periódicos)?

—Pienso separarlos.

2.

—¿Cuándo vas a apagar (la botella / la luz)?

—Voy a apagarla ahora mismo.

3.

—¿Qué vas a hacer con (la bicicleta / la piel)?

—Pues, todavía no sé.

4.

—¿Qué puedo hacer con (la guía telefónica / la revista)?

—Puedes reciclarla.

5.

—¿Qué debo hacer con (el vidrio / el cartón)?

—Hay que separarlo.

6.

—¿Podemos reciclar (el plástico / el aluminio)?

—¡Claro que sí!

7.

—¿Tenemos que reciclar (el cartón / la revista)?

—Sí, pero creo que no vale la pena.

8.

—¿Qué vas a hacer con (las revistas / las bicicletas)?

—Voy a ponerlas con los periódicos.

You are writing an editorial for the local newspaper to try to get the community interested in recycling. In order to give accurate information, you are checking with different families to see what they currently recycle. Complete the dialogues by identifying the pictures. Follow the model.

—¿Qué reciclas tú para proteger la Tierra?

—Reciclo *botellas*.

1.

—¿Qué separan Uds.?

—Separamos _____.

2.

—¿Cómo conservas tú energía?

—Yo conservo energía cuando apago _____.

3.

—¿Tenemos que reciclar _____ en nuestra comunidad?

—Sí, la tenemos que reciclar.

4.

—¿Cómo reducen Uds. la basura?

—Reciclamos _____.

5.

—¿Cómo puedo conservar energía?

—Puedes _____ más a menudo.

6.

—¿Tienes que reciclar _____ en tu comunidad?

—Sí, lo tengo que reciclar.

You are very interested in animals and notice them wherever you go. You wonder if everyone else is as aware of living creatures as you are, so you take a survey to find out. Complete the dialogues by underlining the words that identify the pictures. Follow the model.

—¿Qué viste tú en el zoológico?

—Yo vi (<u>un elefante</u> / una vaca).

1.

—¿Qué vieron Uds. en el árbol?

—Nosotros vimos (un pájaro / una planta).

2.

—¿Qué vio Paula en el océano?

—Paula vio (una ballena / un lobo).

3.

—¿Qué vieron tus padres en el campo?

—Mis padres vieron (un oso / un caballo).

4.

—¿Qué vieron Carmen y tú en la selva?

—Nosotros vimos (una vaca / un jaguar).

5.

—¿Qué viste en la selva?

—Vi (una serpiente / un árbol).

6.

—¿Qué vio Ud. en el zoológico?

—Vi (un gorila / un aire).

7.

—¿Qué vio tu hermano en el campo?

—Vio (una flor / un lobo).

8.

—¿Qué vieron Uds. en el zoológico?

—Vimos (un oso / un tigre).

Your "Save the Earth" group has decided to make sure that the younger children in your community are aware of all the endangered species and other environmental issues. You receive permission to go to the elementary schools to talk to them about your concerns. Complete the dialogues according to the pictures. Follow the model.

—¿Dónde vio *el pájaro* azul Ricardo?

—Ricardo lo vio en *el aire*.

1.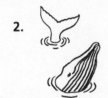

—¿Dónde vieron _____ tus hermanas?

—Ellas la vieron en _____ .

2.

—¿Vieron Uds. _____ en el zoológico?

—No, la vimos en _____ .

3.

—¿Sacaste fotos en las vacaciones?

—Sí, saqué fotos de _____ y

_____ .

4.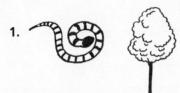

—¿Viste _____ en el parque?

—Sí, las vi y también vi muchas _____ .

5.

—¿Son _____ una amenaza para el

medio ambiente?

—Sí, pero las necesitamos.

6.

—¿Cómo podemos conservar energía?

—Pues, podemos usar _____ .

You are trying to convince your family to set up recycling bins in the basement and to be more interested in saving the environment. You have won over everyone except your older sister. She is one of those people who has to hear everyone else's opinion before she can make up her own mind. First fill in the verb chart. Then complete the dialogues with the correct form of the verb *decir*. Follow the model.

Decir

yo	d- _____	nosotros nosotras	d- _____
tú	d- _____	vosotros vosotras	decís
Ud. él ella	d- _____	Uds. ellos ellas	d- _____

—¿Qué *dice* José de la energía?

—José *dice* que es importante conservar energía.

1. —¿Qué _____ Uds. de las fábricas?

   —Nosotros _____ que las fábricas no son buenas para el medio ambiente.

2. —¿Qué _____ tú del jaguar?

   —Yo _____ que el jaguar está en peligro de extinción.

3. —¿Qué _____ Roberto y Alicia de las latas?

   —Ellos _____ que necesitan reciclarlas.

4. —¿Qué _____ papá de separar el aluminio?

   —Papá _____ que debemos separarlo.

5. —Profesora, ¿qué _____ Ud. de la basura?

   —Yo _____ que es importante reducirla.

6. —¿Qué _____ mamá de las botellas de vidrio?

   —Mamá _____ que debemos separarlas.

7. —¿Qué _____ tú de las luces?

   —Yo _____ que es importante apagarlas.

You and your friends are having a hard time deciding what to do with the rest of your vacation. You've done lots of different things so far, so you start to ask others what else you could do. Complete the verb chart. Then write dialogues based on the pictures using the correct form of the verb *decir*. Follow the model.

Decir

yo	d- _____	nosotros nosotras	d- _____
tú	d- _____	vosotros vosotras	decís
Ud. él ella	d- _____	Uds. ellos ellas	d- _____

Hernán   —¿*Qué dice Hernán?*

—*Hernán dice que debemos estudiar.*

1.   **tus padres**   — _____

   — _____.

2.   **tú**   — _____

   — _____.

3.   **Uds.**   — _____

   — _____.

4.   **ellos**   — _____

   — _____.

5.   **Rosalinda y tú**   — _____

   — _____.

6.   **Mamá**   — _____

   — _____.

Gramática en contexto / El verbo decir   **141**

You are a very disorganized person and today you have a million things to do. You need someone to direct you! Write dialogues according to the pictures. Follow the model.

—¿Qué debo hacer?

—*Lava la ropa y después saca la basura.*

1.

—¿Qué debo hacer?

— _____ .

2.

—¿Qué debo hacer?

— _____ .

3.

—¿Qué debo hacer?

— _____ .

4.

—¿Qué debo hacer?

— _____ .

5.

—¿Qué debo hacer?

— _____ .

6.

—¿Qué debo hacer?

— _____ .

A You and your family have company coming over soon and you have a lot of things to do before they arrive. Your father is assigning tasks to each family member. Complete each dialogue. Follow the model.

—¿Debo lavar el vestido azul?

—*Sí, lávalo por favor.*

1. —¿Debo sacar la basura?

   — _____.

2. —¿Debo sacudir los muebles?

   — _____.

3. —¿Debo poner la mesa?

   — _____.

4. —¿Debo arreglar el cuarto?

   — _____.

5. —¿Debo hacer la cama?

   — _____.

6. —¿Debo limpiar el baño ahora?

   — _____.

7. —¿Debo abrir las ventanas?

   — _____.

B Now that everyone has arrived, see what you can do to make them all comfortable.

 —¿Qué le debo traer a tío Ricardo?

—*Tráele una revista.*

1.  —¿Qué le debo traer a tía Sofía?

   — _____.

2. —¿Qué les debo servir a los primos?

   — _____.

3.  —¿Qué le debo servir a abuelita?

   — _____.

Gramática en contexto / El mandato afirmativo (tú)   **143**

It's a good thing that your class isn't having a test today! Some of you knew all the answers to the questions when you discussed them at the lunch table, but others didn't know a single answer. First fill in the verb chart. Then complete the dialogues according to the clues in parentheses. Follow the model.

Saber

yo	_____	nosotros nosotras	_____
tú	_____	vosotros vosotras	sabéis
Ud. él ella	_____	Uds. ellos ellas	_____

—¿*Sabes* tú esquiar?

—*Yo no sé, pero Alicia sí sabe.* (Alicia)

1. —¿ _____ Uds. patinar?

   — _____ . (Roberto y Raúl)

2. —¿ _____ Ud. cuándo llega el tren?

   — _____ . (el profesor)

3. —¿ _____ Rosa dónde está el libro de español?

   — _____ . (yo)

4. —¿ _____ tus primos jugar fútbol?

   — _____ . (Pablo y yo)

5. —¿ _____ tú dónde vive la hermana de Luis?

   — _____ . (Marta y Concha)

6. —¿ _____ Uds. adónde podemos llevar las latas?

   — _____ . (Marcos)

7. —¿ _____ Ud. cuánto cuestan estos zapatos?

   — _____ . (ella)

8. —¿ _____ Julia tocar la guitarra?

   — _____ . (mi hermana)

9. —¿ _____ tus padres jugar tenis?

   — _____ . (mis hermanos)

CAPÍTULO 13

You seem to have lost your memory and your sense of direction! You have to go to a nearby town tomorrow, but you're not sure where different things are located. You ask everyone in your family and your friends at school for directions. Complete the verb chart. Then write dialogues according to the pictures and the clues provided. Follow the model.

	Saber	Decir
yo	_____	_____
tú	_____	_____
él / ella / Ud.	_____	_____
nosotros / nosotras	_____	_____
vosotros / vosotras	sabéis	decís
ellos / ellas / Uds.	_____	_____

—¿Sabe Juan dónde está el banco?

—Sí, dice que está cerca de la biblioteca.

Juan   **cerca de**

1.

tus padres   **al lado de**

—¿ _____ ?

— _____ .

2.

Uds.   **lejos de**

—¿ _____ ?

— _____ .

3.

tú   **a la derecha**

—¿ _____ ?

— _____ .

4.

Carlota y Eva   **enfrente de**

—¿ _____ ?

— _____ .

Paso a paso 1

CAPÍTULO 13

Nombre _____

Fecha _____

**Practice Workbook
Organizer**

I. Vocabulary

Conservation words	Recyclable items	Animals
_____	_____	_____
_____	_____	_____
_____	_____	_____
_____	_____	_____

Nature / environment words	Environmental dangers	Transportation words
_____	_____	_____
_____	_____	_____
_____	_____	_____
_____	_____	_____

II. Grammar

1. The verb *to say:* _____ .

S	P
_____	_____
_____	decís
_____	_____

2. The affirmative *tú* command form for regular and stem-changing verbs is the same as the

_____ and _____ form of the present tense.

3. The verb *to know:* _____ .

S	P
_____	_____
_____	sabéis
_____	_____

4. _____ + infinitive means _____ .

It must be the season for parties! Everyone at school is talking about gatherings and reunions. What present are you giving? Who's coming? What are you serving? Complete each dialogue by underlining the words that identify the picture. Follow the model.

—¿Qué traes a (<u>la fiesta de cumpleaños</u> / una reunión) para Mercedes?

—Traigo un regalo hecho a mano.

1.
—¿Qué vas a servir en (la fiesta de la escuela / la fiesta de disfraces)?

—Voy a servir churros y chocolate.

2.
—¿A quiénes vas a invitar a (la fiesta de fin de año / la fiesta de sorpresa)?

—Voy a invitar a mis amigas Paula, Alicia y Ana.

3.
—¿Con quién vas a (la fiesta de fin de año / la reunión)?

—Voy con Ramón y Teresa.

4.
—¿A qué hora empieza (el baile / la fiesta de la escuela)?

—Empieza a las ocho.

5.
—¿Con quién vas a la fiesta, con (tu novio / tu hermana)?

—Pues, todavía no sé.

6.
—¿Cuándo es (la fiesta de disfraces / el baile) de primavera?

—Creo que es en el mes de mayo.

A You and your mother are trying to make plans for some upcoming parties. Complete each dialogue by identifying the pictures. Follow the model.

—¿Vas a invitar a María a tu *fiesta de cumpleaños?*

—Ya la invité ayer.

1.

—¿Adónde vas mañana?

—Voy a la _____ .

2.

—¿Qué van a servir Uds. en la _____ ?

—Vamos a servir hamburguesas, tacos y enchiladas.

3.

—¿Qué sueles regalarle a tu _____ ?

—Suelo regalarle regalos hechos a mano.

B In the middle of a conversation you are having with your mother, your brother arrives with a friend. Complete the conversation using the words from the word bank.

encantada	alguien	te presento	conoces	cantar	novia

1. —¡Hola, Mercedes! _____ a mi amigo Jaime.

2. —¡ _____ , Jaime! ¿Cómo estás?

3. —Muy bien, gracias. ¿Conoces a mi _____ , Gloria? Ella va

a _____ en la fiesta de Juan este fin de semana.

4. —¡Sí, claro que la conozco! Es _____ con mucho talento.

Neither you nor your friends can stop talking about the elegant New Year's Eve party that José's family is giving this year. Complete the conversations by underlining the words that identify the pictures. Follow the model.

—No sé qué voy a llevar a la fiesta.

—Pues, ¿por qué no llevas (el vestido de fiesta / <u>los zapatos de tacón alto</u>)?

1.

—¿Qué vas a llevar con el vestido de fiesta?

—Voy a llevar (el reloj pulsera / el collar).

2.

—¿Qué llevaste a la fiesta del año pasado?

—Llevé (un traje / una corbata).

3.

—¿Vas a ayudar a José?

—Sí, voy a ayudarlo a (decorar / preparar).

4.

—Necesito comprar algo para llevar con este vestido.

—Pues, ¿por qué no llevas estos (aretes / joyas)?

5.

—¿Qué vas a regalarle a Antonio por su cumpleaños?

—Voy a comprarle un (collar / reloj pulsera).

6.

—No sé qué llevar con estos aretes.

—¿Por qué no llevas una (corbata / pulsera) de oro?

7.

—¿Hay que llevar traje a la fiesta de etiqueta?

—Claro que sí, y debes llevar (una corbata / un collar) también.

A You have arrived late to the party. You pull your best friend aside and ask her lots of questions about what happened before you arrived. Complete each conversation by identifying the picture. Follow the model.

—¿Qué le compró Roberto a Anita?

—Le compró *un collar.*

1.

—¿Por qué te duelen los pies?

—Me duelen porque llevo _____.

2.

—No veo a Pablo. ¿Está aquí?

—Sí, él lleva _____ gris.

3.

—¿Qué le regalaste a Noemí?

—Le regalé _____.

4.

—¿Vas a comprar algo para llevar con tu vestido largo?

—Sí, compré _____ nueva.

B Your friend then starts to tell you that things aren't going very well at this party. Complete the following dialogue by choosing words from the word bank.

| pasarlo bien | bailando | comiendo | escoger | ambiente |

1. —¡El _____ de esta fiesta es muy aburrido!

2. —Los invitados no están _____ . ¿Por qué?

3. —Creo que no les gusta la comida. Ellos no están _____ tampoco.

4. —Voy a _____ otra clase de música.

5. —Sí, por favor, porque yo quiero _____ .

A Your brother is in a very bad mood, and he insists on saying the opposite of everything you say. First fill in the chart. Then complete each dialogue by using the expression that means the opposite. Follow the model.

Positive	Negative
_____ something	_____ nothing
_____ someone	_____ nobody
_____ always	_____ never

—Voy a dar algo a Ricardo por su cumpleaños. ¿Y Mateo?

—*Mateo no le va a dar nada por su cumpleaños.*

1. —Yo siempre saco fotos en las vacaciones. ¿Y tú?

    — _____ .

2. —Alicia bailó con alguien ayer en la fiesta. ¿Y Pablo y Ana?

    — _____ .

3. —Yo no estudio con nadie hoy. ¿Y tú?

    — _____ .

4. —Catalina nunca visita a su abuelita. ¿Y sus hermanas?

    — _____ .

5. —Óscar no va a comer nada en el almuerzo. ¿Y Ernesto?

    — _____ .

B Now see if you can remember how to use the expressions *tampoco*, *también*, and *ni... ni* from earlier in the book.

1. —No me gusta estudiar. ¿Y a ti?

    —No, _____ .

2. —A Rafael no le gusta bailar. A Julio no le gusta cantar. ¿Y a ti?

    —No, _____ .

3. —Me gusta cocinar. ¿Y a Ud.?

    —Sí, _____ .

Gramática en contexto / Construcciones negativas   **151**

CAPÍTULO 14

Your ride to the party was late! You've just arrived and now you are wondering what all of your friends are doing. First fill in the chart. Then complete each dialogue according to the verb in parentheses. Follow the model.

Present progressive

estoy	bail _____		estamos	bail _____
	com _____			com _____
	escrib _____			escrib _____
estás	bail _____		estáis	bail _____
	com _____			com _____
	escrib _____			escrib _____
está	bail _____		están	bail _____
	com _____			com _____

—¿Qué están haciendo Raúl y Jorge? (cantar)

—*Ellos están cantando.*

1. —¿Qué está haciendo Óscar? (bailar)

   — _____ .

2. —¿Qué estás haciendo tú? (comer)

   — _____ .

3. —¿Qué están haciendo Uds.? (hablar)

   — _____ .

4. —¿Qué está haciendo Ud.? (sacar fotos)

   — _____ .

5. —¿Qué están haciendo Norma y Olga? (ver la televisión)

   — _____ .

6. —¿Qué está haciendo Beatriz? (poner la mesa)

   — _____ .

Your family is having a reunion at a resort in Puerto Rico! There is so much to do! First fill in the chart. Then write dialogues according to the words in parentheses. Follow the model.

Present progressive

estoy	*bail* _____	estamos	*bail* _____
	com _____		*com* _____
	escrib _____		*escrib* _____
estás	*bail* _____	estáis	*bail* _____
	com _____		*com* _____
	escrib _____		*escrib* _____
está	*bail* _____	están	*bail* _____
	com _____		*com* _____

(Juan / descansar / nadar)   —*¿Está descansando Juan?*

—*No, Juan está nadando.*

1. **(tú / comer / bailar)** —¿ _____ ?

   — _____ .

2. **(Eva y Alfonso / depositar dinero / enviar una carta)** —¿ _____

   _____ ?

   — _____ .

3. **(Uds. / sacar un libro / devolver un libro)** —¿ _____

   _____ ?

   — _____ .

4. **(Clara / cantar / decorar la sala)** —¿ _____ ?

   — _____ .

5. **(Ester y tú / dibujar / jugar tenis)** —¿ _____

   _____ ?

   — _____ .

Five students in your class will celebrate their birthdays this month. Everyone is talking about what gifts they are going to give to them. First fill in the verb chart. Then complete the dialogues according to the model.

Dar

yo	_____	nosotros nosotras	_____
tú	_____	vosotros vosotras	dais
Ud. él ella	_____	Uds. ellos ellas	_____

—¿Qué le das a Diego por su cumpleaños?

—*Le doy a Diego una corbata. ¿Y Eva?*

—*Eva va a darle un reloj pulsera.*

1.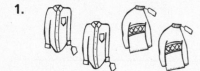

—¿Qué les dan Uds. a las gemelas?

— _____ . ¿Y tú?

— _____ .

2.

—¿Qué les das a Sergio y Sonia?

— _____ . ¿Y Gerardo?

— _____ .

3.

—¿Qué le damos a Luz?

— _____ . ¿Y tú?

— _____ .

4.

—¿Qué les da a sus padres?

— _____ . ¿Y Uds.?

— _____ .

Everyone is talking about giving gifts. But some of you are feeling very stingy and you aren't giving anything! First fill in the verb chart. Then complete the dialogues by using the correct form of the verb *dar* and the word in parentheses to finish the question and to write a negative response. Follow the model.

Dar

yo	_____	nosotros nosotras	_____
tú	_____	vosotros vosotras	dais
Ud. él ella	_____	Uds. ellos ellas	_____

—¿*Da* Ud. un regalo a su hermana por su cumpleaños? (nunca)

—*Nunca le doy un regalo a mi hermana.*

1. —¿ _____ Uds. un collar a su amiga? (nada)

   — _____ .

2. —¿ _____ Javier un sombrero a tu primo? (nadie)

   — _____ .

3. —¿ _____ tú los aretes a tu hermana? (nada)

   — _____ .

4. —¿ _____ tus padres un regalo a tu novia? (nunca)

   — _____ .

5. —¿ _____ Andrés un regalo a Luis? (nunca)

   — _____ .

6. —¿ _____ tus amigos un regalo hecho a mano a José? (nadie)

   — _____ .

7. —¿ _____ yo una corbata a Ignacio? (nada)

   — _____ .

I. Vocabulary

Words to talk about parties	Words to introduce people

Words to talk about clothes	Words to talk about gift-giving

II. Grammar

1. There are two ways to make a sentence negative. If the negative word comes after the verb, put _____ or _____ .

2. The negative words are:

   _____ (neither...nor)   _____ (never)   _____ (nobody)

   _____ (neither)   _____ (nothing)

3. We use the present progressive tense to _____ .

4. To form the present progressive, use the present tense of _____ + _____ .

5. To form the present participle, drop the *-ar* from *-ar* verbs and add _____ , and drop the *-er* and *-ir* from *-er* and *-ir* verbs and add _____ .

6. The verb *to give:* _____ .

S	P
_____	_____
_____	dais
_____	_____